SOUPY SEZ!

SOUPY SEZ!

My Zany Life and Times

SOUPY SALES

WITH CHARLES SALZBERG

M. EVANS AND COMPANY, INC.
NEW YORK

M. Evans and Company, Inc.
216 East 49th Street
New York, New York 10017

Library of Congress Cataloging-in-Publication Data

Sales, Soupy.
    Soupy sez! : my zany life and times / by Soupy Sales with Charles Salzberg.
      p. cm.
    ISBN 0-87131-935-7
    1. Sales, Soupy. 2. Comedians—United States—Biograghy. I. Salzberg, Charles. II. Title.
PN2287.S26 A3 2001
792.7'028'092—dc21
   [B]   2001040767

Typesetting and book design by Evan H. Johnston

Printed in the United States of America

9 8 7 6 5 4 3 2 1

Dedicated to
Adelaide Nimitz-Factor,
Clyde Adler,
John Pival,
WXYZ-TV in Detroit,
and to my family, my
friends, and above all—
my fans.

CONTENTS

SOUPY'S SCORECARD

Over the years, I've worked a lot of different shows in a lot of different cities to a lot of different audiences. Sometimes my shows have confused people because the names have been the same, even though they might have been in different cities in different years at different times. Hell, sometimes I'm even confused myself. In any case, just so you can get a better handle on my career, I've decided to present you with this easy-to-read-chart of my television career.

Cincinnati
WKRC, a CBS affiliate
Soupy's Soda Shop, 1950–1951, 5:30–6:30 P.M. Mon.–Fri.
Club Nothing, 1950–1951, 10:45 P.M.–12:00 A.M. Mon.–Fri.

Cleveland
WXEL, independent station
Soupy's On 1951–1952, 11:30 A.M.–12:00 P.M., Mon.–Fri.

Detroit
WXYZ, an ABC affiliate
12 o'clock Comics, 1953, 12:30. 1:00 P.M. Mon–Fri.
Lunch With Soupy (the name of *12 o'clock Comics* was changed to this name after a couple of months), 1953–1960. The name was changed to *Breakfast with Soupy* when, for a while, they changed the time of the show to 8:00 o'clock in the morning.
Soupy's On, 1953 (a few months after I arrived at the station), 11:00–11:15 P.M. (after a few months the show was extended, running from 11:00–11:30 P.M.)
Soupy's Ranch, 1955–1956, Wednesdays, 8:00 P.M.–9:00 P.M.

ABC-TV
The Soupy Sales Show (winter replacement for *Kukla, Fran and Ollie*), 1955, 7:00–7:15 P.M.
The Soupy Sales Show 1957–1960 12:00 P.M.–12:30 P.M., Saturdays.

KABC-Los Angeles
The Soupy Sales Show, 1961
The Soupy Sales Show, 1962, 7:30–8:00 P.M., Fridays.

WNEW-New York
The Soupy Sales Show, 1964–1966, various times, Mon–Fri. (syndicated show 1965–1966)

Syndicated Show
The New Soupy Sales Show, 1979, various times, Mon–Fri.

PART I

THE EARLY YEARS

SOUPY SEZ

Show me England being invaded by toads and I'll show you a froggy day in London town.

WHTN Radio publicity photo, Huntington, 1946.

I

THe PRiNCe IS BORN aND NOt a Pie IN SiGHt

FRaNKLiNtoN, NC, 1926–1933
HuNtiNGton, WV, 1934–1949

I got my genes from my grandmother. On her 76th birthday the doctor told her to run five miles a day. Now she's 94 and we don't know where the hell she is.

• • •

I guess I might as well start from the beginning, since starting anywhere else doesn't make a whole lot of sense unless, of course, you're reading this from back to front.

I was born in Franklinton, North Carolina—primarily because I wanted to be near my mother. Franklinton, which wasn't far from Wake Forest University, was a small, sleepy town with a population of fifteen hundred, and that number never changed. Every time a baby was born, some guy left town. Coincidence? I don't think so.

Being a small town, there wasn't much to do around Franklinton, which probably explains why my mother gave birth four times—and not all of them were me. The first born, Marvin, died in childhood; then there was Leonard; followed a few years later by Jack, and then there was me, Milton, yes, Milton. Do you honestly think anyone would actually name their son, *Soupy?*—That name came later.

My parents, Irving and Sadie Supman, came to Franklinton after World War I and opened up a dry goods business called the Wonder Department Store—and if you're wondering what dry goods are in relation to wet goods, you're wondering the same thing as I am. And if you're wondering why they wound up in Franklinton, so am I, because if it weren't for bowling, Franklinton wouldn't have had any culture at all.

My mother and father were both born in Baltimore, Maryland. In fact, they were both born on the same day, the Fourth of July, but my father was ten years older than my mother, so it wasn't really the *same* day, was it? My mother was always bragging about the fact that both she and my father were July fourth, Independence Day babies and wasn't that something special? Finally, one day when I was sick of hearing about it, I said to my mother, "Well, why didn't you marry Louis Armstrong? He was also born on July fourth."

When they met and got married, my father was working in Baltimore, but because his brother had a store in Raleigh, North Carolina, he decided to pack up and move down there to seek his fortune (the fame part was going to be left to me). Eventually, he moved to Franklinton and opened up his own store.

I arrived in the world on January 8, 1926, under the sign of Capricorn (I bet you thought I was going to say a stop sign, huh?). Nothing ever comes easy for Capricorns, or so I'm told, and this certainly turned out to be true for me. My brothers already had their nicknames in place when I made my appearance: Leonard was Hambone and Jack was Chickenbone, so the only thing left for me was Soupbone, which believe me, was a lot better than Milkbone. Besides, down south everyone pronounced our last name *Soup*man instead of *Sup*man, so "Soupy" seemed very appropriate. I didn't mind, just so long as they didn't call me late for dinner.

I think growing up in the South affected my personality because

I was brought up during a time when there was a lot of prejudice, much more than there is now, and being an observant kid, I couldn't help but see what was happening around me. I believe that observing this and taking it in made me a much better person. Years later, when I read Harper Lee's *To Kill a Mockingbird*, I really identified with those kids in their innocence and their lack of prejudice, even as horrible things were taking place around them.

It was a time when the Ku Klux Klan was a dominant and deadly force in the South. Fortunately, they never bothered us—probably because my father was the one who sold them their sheets. They even invited him to join the Klan, but for obvious reasons he turned them down. Back then racism was an accepted way of life, simply part of the social fabric. As a young child, I was blissfully unaware of it—that is, until a horrifying event took place when I was about seven years old, the aftermath of which I'll never forget. To this day, I still have nightmares about it.

Like most every public place in the south, the movie theater in town—the only movie theater in town, I should add—was segregated. Black people could attend, but they were made to sit upstairs in the balcony. One steamy summer night the manager, Mr. Brown, who lived in our neighborhood and had five daughters, discovered that a black gentleman was breaking the house rules by smoking during the show. When Mr. Brown ordered the man out of the theater, a violent altercation ensued, which wound up tragically with the black patron throwing Mr. Brown off the balcony to his death. Naturally, the patron was arrested and thrown in jail. But he never made it to court. A couple of days later, I was walking through the center of town and there he was, or what was left of him, hanging from a telephone pole for everyone to see. After they'd lynched him, the KKK had stuck a cigarette between his lifeless lips, just to get their point across in case anyone had missed it. This gruesome spectacle left an indelible, lifelong impression on me. I can still see that man swinging from that telephone pole with that cigarette butt dangling from his mouth, as vividly as if it all happened just last week.

In many ways, for those first years of my life, I led an idyllic childhood. In fact, if I had to choose just one memory to keep, even with all the success I've had, I think it would probably be a memory from childhood, especially a memory of me and my father, who died when I was very young.

One thing I got from my parents (other than my name, of course) is a love for others. They loved everybody and taught us to do the same. Even today, what with all I've been through, I think I'm still the same way. Another thing I inherited from my mother and father is a trusting nature, and I'm afraid that has caused some problems for me along the way. If I were asked what characteristic I would hope my two boys, Tony and Hunt, haven't inherited from me, I would say the inclination to believe what everybody tells them. After all these years—finally—I've learned that you've got to have a healthy dose of skepticism to get along in the world.

My father died of tuberculosis when I was only five years old, so I hardly knew him, not only because he died so young, but also because he was always working long hours in the store, hardly ever around the house. In fact, sadly, I have only a few vague memories of him and, interestingly enough, all of them took place in his store. I remember one time my mother and I were going up to Raleigh for a birthday party and I was all dressed up and ready to go, waiting for my mother to get ready, and my father bent over, patted me on the head, and said gently, "Be a good boy, Soupy." I looked up at him and said, "Okay." And I was a good boy, at least for a while.

When my father passed away, he was only forty-one years old. Nobody came up to me and said, "Hey, your dad died." I didn't even get to go to the funeral. That just wasn't the way they did things in those days. I guess they figured kids couldn't handle death and so it was better just to ignore it and make believe that my father was just on a very, very long business trip. His death affected me very much, because after that, I didn't really have much of a family life. He was buried in Baltimore, and that's where my mother was buried, too, right beside him, when she died in 1970 at the age of seventy-four.

It wasn't easy for my mother, bringing up three boys, but she did a damn good job of it. She was a strong woman and I probably inherited my sense of humor from her. I remember she'd come back from playing cards with her friends and she'd say to me, "Everyone says how funny I am," and I'd say, "Okay, what did you say that was so funny?" She'd say, "I don't know, but everybody said it was funny." I guess I had to take her word for it.

About a year after my father died, when I was six years old, I made my stage debut playing the title role in my elementary school production of "Peter Rabbit." It was, without doubt, the pivotal event of my life, because when I heard those two hundred or so people laughing and clapping when I made my grand entrance from a barrel and then sang a song, I felt like a bolt of lightening had struck me. To this day, I think that the thing that makes me happiest is the applause and laughter I get from an audience. And the thing that probably makes me unhappiest is the reality that you can't work all of the time, which means that the applause and laughter is limited to the time you're actually performing. I know all you amateur head shrinkers out there are probably nodding your heads and saying, "Well, that's why he's in show business today. He needs constant reassurance, constant demonstrations of love." And the truth is, you may be right. I am a workaholic. But I also love to entertain people. I love to make them smile. And even if I'd listened to my parents and become an optician, I suspect I'd be a very funny one.

Anyway, I don't know whether it was a message from God or not, but after that gig as Peter Rabbit, I said to myself, "Soupy, this is what you're going to do with your life." It's weird, I know, because I was only six years old, and yet somehow I knew that entertaining people was going to be my life.

I once asked Frank Sinatra if talent was hereditary or a special individual God-given trait. He said, "Well, Soupy, your two brothers aren't in show business." He felt that people like us were put here on this earth to entertain people and make them happy. And listen, I wasn't about to go up against Frank, or else I'd probably wind up being a right turn on Route 95.

Once my father died, I wound up spending a lot of time by myself. My brothers were older and, like most older siblings, didn't pay too much attention to me. My mother, now the sole wage earner, spent most of her day working. My mother would leave the house at seven in the morning and come home at seven at night. On Saturdays, I'd go to the movies and spend the whole day there. I'd be half asleep when my mother would come and pick me up and take me home.

I loved the movies. They gave me a taste of what I thought my life was going to be like when I grew up. I was going to be a performer, just like those folks up on the silver screen, which was going to be a way for me to relate to other people. And, in my own small way, even as a child, that's exactly what I did—perform.

· · ·

Huntington has a great device for removing snow. It's called July.

· · ·

Our family remained in Franklinton for a few years after my father died, but it was rough on my mother, running the store alone and all. Eventually, she met a traveling salesman (not *that* traveling salesman) from West Virginia, named Felix Goldstein. They were married in 1934. He was much older than my mother and already had two sons, one of whom was a doctor and the other was studying to be a dentist.

After my mother remarried, we moved from Franklinton and settled in Huntington, West Virginia, the place I still think of as my hometown. I love the place. It's where my roots are, where my first experiences in life were and my best friends still live. I grew up there and I plan to be buried there . . . when I die, of course. Before that would be a little premature, don't you think?

I took to Huntington like a duck to water, and I guess Huntington took to me, too, because today the city is proud to claim me as one of their own. I know this is true because in the center of town, near the municipal complex, the town fathers erected and dedicated the Soupy Sales Plaza, where I still go once a year, usually in the month of June, to perform a free comedy and music show. At the same time, I get a chance to visit with the many friends I have who still live there. Even today, I have very strong emotional ties to Huntington. It doesn't make any difference where I am or what I'm doing; when I think of home—and believe me, over the years I've had a lot of them—I think of Huntington. It's where I spent the happiest years of my life, and sometimes I wake up and I just know I've got to go back there.

And yet, I think that growing up in a small town limited me somewhat in terms of my career. Perhaps it had something to do with being unprepared for the kinds of people I was going to meet in the business, the kinds of people who didn't know how to be straight with you, the kinds of people whose only interest in you would be what you could do for them. I think the one thing I like least about show business is the fact that there are a lot of people in our business who do not stick up for, or try to help, other people in the business, whether they're trying to get a break, climbing up the ladder, or having a difficult time. Throughout my career, I've tried to be as generous and kind as I possibly could to everyone. In fact— I know this sounds corny—but it's the truth; my motto is, was, and always will be, "Do unto others as you would have them do unto you."

When I finally did get out into the world, the thing I remember being the most difficult for me was to adapt myself to people other than those I knew in my hometown. I mean, people in clubs and other cities in other areas of the country didn't know me, and because they didn't know me I had to make it solely on the basis of being a performer and entertaining them enough so that they would accept me.

I was very excited about moving, because where I'd come from the main street ran through a car wash. Now, in a bigger town, I figured there'd actually be things to do, places to see.

CHARLIE COOK, SOUPY'S CHILDHOOD FRIEND:

Huntington really was a small town and this story kind of proves that. I remember one time Soupy was standing on the corner waiting for a bus. This was back in the early forties and we were just coming out of the Depression and there weren't many cars around, so we rode the bus. Anyway, he's standing there and a lady comes out of the house in front of which he was standing, comes over to him, and asks, "Are you Soupy?" And he says, "Yes." She says, "Well, you're wanted on the telephone." And then she invites him inside. It was a friend of ours, Bill Young, who said, "Hey, where ya goin'?" "Downtown," said Soupy. "Well, I'll meet you down there." Evidently, Bill, who was a little wacky himself, had called Soupy's house and his mother had told him where Soupy was and he just found the woman's name and number and called her up and described Soupy and asked her to look outside for him. What was really amazing was that the woman just let him in. But that's just the way it was back in those days.

· · ·

Huntington was always a very social town. They even had fraternities and sororities in high school. We had great dances and, unlike today when every day is casual Friday, everybody dressed up. We had great events like the Beau Brummel Ball, and places like Amsbary Johnson's, Dunhill's, Angel's, and Foard & Harwood would donate clothes. Everybody would plan for months to go to the Beau Brummel Ball and nobody would tell anyone what they were going to wear.

All in all, those were terrific times back in Huntington, and I wouldn't trade them for anything. And the friends I made back then are still very much in my life.

CHARLIE COOK:

Soupy and I both moved to Huntington when we were in the fourth grade, and we wound up living in the same neighborhood, so we became best friends. We went all through high school and a couple of years of college at Marshall together, and then I attended pharmacy school in Cincinnati while Soupy began his career in show business, which didn't surprise me at all, considering some of the things we did when we were kids.

There are lots of stories I could tell about Soupy, but a few in particular stand out. One of them took place back in the early '40s, around Christmastime. Soupy and I found we didn't have any money, which wasn't all that unusual for us, so, we came up with this scheme to have a turkey raffle. We had the tickets printed up and we talked the Clique Club at the high school into selling them for ten cents a chance to win a fifteen-pound turkey. We were going to have the drawing in the lobby of Frederick's hotel, which was the biggest hotel in town, only we didn't bother to inform the hotel that we were gonna do that. Well, Saturday morning comes and there's a hotel lobby full of kids; gosh, we must have sold several hundred tickets, and when we drew the winning guy's name we asked him if he wanted the turkey or the money prize, which we pegged at five dollars. He said, "You can't buy a fif-teen-pound turkey for five dollars." And we said, "If it's alive, you can." He said, "I'm not taking a live turkey, I'll take the five bucks." We made about fifteen bucks apiece that day, and by the time the hotel figured out what was going on, we'd high-tailed it out of there.

• • •

BiLL CRAVENS, CHiLDHOOD FRiEND FROM HUNTiNGTON:

Soupy moved into our neighborhood in the summer of 1934 and we became close friends, and our friendship lasted all through high school and college. In fact, I was best man at his first wedding.

I remember, when we were kids, maybe nine or ten years old, we used to put on shows for the neighborhood kids in his garage. I was the straight man and he was the comedian. We charged a penny and we even had a sideshow that we put on. We had one kid from the neighborhood, Otis Cavendish, who could drink down a bottle of pop without moving his Adam's apple. He was quite a draw.

In high school Soupy used to send his joke material to comedians like Bob Hope and Red Skelton. I'm not sure he ever had anything pur-chased, but that didn't stop him from sending them out anyway. He was also a big band expert to the point where he could tell you who played every instrument in every band.

I was also on the high school newspaper with him—and we both wrote about sports. I was on the basketball and track team and little Soupy was the track manager. One of his duties was to keep the broad-jump pit, which was filled with sawdust, all fluffed up so that the athletes wouldn't hurt themselves. One time, during practice, Jack Jenkins, the star broadjumper, broke his ankle and the coach blamed it on poor Soupy for not keeping that pit properly fluffed up. The track team would travel to other schools for meets and Soupy and I had this special sign language thing so that in the car we'd be laughing all the time, till it came to a point where the coach wanted to throw us out of the car.

• • •

I was an inveterate class cutup, but I don't think you could consider me the class clown. If you ask me, I just think I had a little more personality than most people. And maybe that's why I was voted the most popular kid in school. Or maybe it was all those free sodas I handed out to the voters. Okay, why beat around the bush? I guess I was a pretty funny guy for around there—after all, we're talking about Huntington, West Virginia, which isn't exactly Las Vegas, is it? But, let's face it, if you look like I did then you had to be funny. Speaking of looks, someone once asked me if there was a physical feature I would change and I said, yes, I would like to have another nose—not two noses, just another one other than the one I have.

I also played a few pranks that got me a little attention (sometimes more than a little). For instance, I once gradually whittled down the bottoms of two canes that were used by one of the older teachers at school until one afternoon the guy ran screaming into the hall, "I'm taller! I'm taller!" But of course, there were other stories about me that floated around that weren't true. For instance, no matter what anyone says I never did try to get a goat onto the roof of the high school—although I did try to get a couple of girls to go up there with me.

BILL CRAVENS:

Soupy was well-known among the kids at school. He was popular and a good dancer. As teenagers, Soupy and I used to double-date all the time, and I recall one night we stayed up all night trying to list all the girls we'd dated. I believe we came up with over 100 different girls, and since I used to have a steady girl most of the time, most of the girls on the list were Soupy's.

I remember one night we were on a double-date and after we did whatever we'd do—go to a movie, go dancing, whatever—we'd go over to the park for some, uh, extracurricular activities. The girl he was with didn't want to go. She said she didn't feel that well. Anyway, after we'd finish over in the park, we'd usually go to get something to eat. But this time, it was obvious that we were taking this girl home, and so she said, "Aren't we going to get something to eat?" And Soupy said, "If you're too sick to neck, you're too sick to eat."

. . .

Like most kids, I was movie mad, and during those early days I became a lifelong aficionado of the western serials, especially those starring Buck Jones, Bob Steele, and Johnny Mack Brown. But from the movies I also absorbed some of the influences that would shape my comedic style as an adult: the anarchic mayhem of the Marx Brothers and, in particular, the zany slapstick antics of the Ritz Brothers, especially Harry Ritz, who was the leader of the trio. And then there were Laurel and Hardy, who also had a big influence on me. I especially admired the physicality of the Marx Brothers and the Ritz Brothers. Physical comedy was always appealing to me because I was feeling very physical in those days and, when you think about it, this was and is a very physical country (and, if you recall, a good deal of my comedy had a physical component to it— I was always moving around, sliding back and forth, falling down).

The movies were pretty much *it* in terms of entertainment. Certainly, there were no nightclubs in North Carolina or West Virginia. And in those days, it seemed to us that nobody went into show business unless you lived in New York or Hollywood, or maybe in Chicago, which played a big part in the early days of both radio and television. But it's different today. You can be in Youngstown, Ohio, or Kalamazoo, Michigan, and find a comedy club to work in. They're everywhere. Nick's grocery store, down the street, is featuring the hottest comic in town. And Tony, the town barber, tells a pretty mean joke, too.

Once I entered high school, I started to channel my performing urges by appearing in plays and, because I loved music, especially the big bands, I even took up the clarinet. But I didn't really like to practice—I was much too busy doing other things—which meant that I wasn't going to grow up to be Benny Goodman (or even play him in the movies—that was left to Steve Allen).

So it was in high school that I really started to get interested in performing and I fell in love with standup comedy. Of course, I had no idea how to write an act, so I got my routines from books, like the ones Bob Hope used to come out with. I'd take jokes from those books and create a routine for myself—okay, so I'd steal bits, but that's the way I learned timing and delivery, by reading those books, listening to the radio, and going to movies. I even remember a couple of the first jokes I ever told. I'd stand up there and I'd say, "My mother and father are in the iron and steel business. My mother irons and my father steals." And here's another one: "I was the teacher's pet—she couldn't afford a dog." People would laugh, and that, of course, just encouraged me to do more of it. It also gave me the confidence I needed once it came time to take my act on the road.

BETTY ANN KEEN, CHILDHOOD FRIEND FROM HUNTINGTON:

Soupy and I went to school together from the time we were in first grade all the way through high school. And you know, when I take a look back at those early school pictures and I see his face I have to laugh because I see that even back then he looks just like a little Soupy.

Soupy and I shared an interest in show business, although the difference between us was I didn't want to be in it, I just adored it, and Soupy always wanted to be a part of it. We were both fans of the big bands and of the kind of music they played. I remember, we had a friend who had a vast record collection, with all the music of the day, and Soupy was so in awe of that. He really knew his music, then and now. In fact, we formed a fan club for the Jerry Wald Orchestra—he was a clarinetist in the 1940s, which, since that's the instrument Soupy played, was probably one of the reasons he had an affinity for him. Soupy and I became the National president and vice president, but of course that was because there was no one else in the fan club.

When Soupy went on to Detroit and had his TV show, I kind of lost track of him. He was just someone I would see on television, someone I used to know, but when he came back to Huntington for a high school reunion a few years ago, we picked up our friendship just where we left off. We had so many laughs and so much fun. It wasn't until he actually got off the plane that I realized I hadn't seen him in so many years and I wondered if he'd remember me. Of course, he did. He remembers everybody. He really puts himself out there and for whatever reason—it's genuine, no one could exhaust themselves so much and show such care for people and places if they didn't genuinely have this feeling of affection.

I remember another time my husband and I went up to New York for a visit and we met up with Soupy. We were walking down the street and, believe it or not, all the hookers came out of the woodwork, saying, "Hi, Soupy." "Hi, Soupy." I turned to him and said, "Soupy, how do they all know you so well?" We all had a good laugh about that one.

. . .

During those high school years, besides trying to perform as much as I could, I also wrote for the school newspaper, reviewing movies and bands, things like that. I was very serious about those reviews because the movies were serious business to me. I took to journalism in a big way, especially sports writing, and when I applied to college I planned to major in journalism. But in fact, I was just biding time, because I knew newspapermen didn't make any money. Show business was what I really loved—being on stage and having people applaud and laugh at me. But I believe that if I hadn't gotten into show business, and if I couldn't have become a cowboy like my childhood heroes, then I probably would have ended up as a writer.

In 1943, I graduated Huntington High and then enrolled in Marshall College, now Marshall University. The commute was pretty easy, since the campus was right there in Huntington. At Marshall, I was known as "Suppy" Supman and I soon got a job writing for the *Parthenon*, the student newspaper. I was assigned to cover intramural sports, but I kept skipping the events and instead went dancing at the Shawkey Student Union, where I'd pass through, grab a quick dance, and then go to class. It wasn't long before they caught on to me at the paper and I was fired by the sports editor, Ernie Salvatore, who told me I was spending too much time delivering punch lines and not enough time collecting bylines.

But there were no hard feelings and later Ernie hired me back, and he and I teamed up to do a radio show. Ernie was the straight man and I did the jokes. As Ernie once said, "Soupy was always cracking me up. He was crazy." And I guess I was.

ERNIE SALVATORE, COLLEGE FRIEND, AND A REPORTER FOR THE HERALD DISPATCH FOR 50 YEARS:

I met Soupy right after the war, when I returned to college. Actually, I caught up to Soupy and his group, because they were really just starting school.

What I remember most about Soupy was that he had a great head of hair and he was always "on." You could always find him over at the student union telling jokes, dancing—he was a great fan of swing dancing in those years.

He was a very good friend of my wife-to-be, whose name was Joanne Pinckard. Actually, she and Soupy even dated a few times. I remember once Soupy was on a date with Joanne, whose father was the Sunday editor over at the paper. It was a foursome and the other fellow, Jimmy Woods, drove Soupy over to Oakwood Road in Huntington to drop him off at Joanne's house, while the other guy was going to get his date and then come back and pick up Soupy. Well, Soupy knocked on the door, someone answered it and he was invited to come inside. So, he sits there in the living room, chatting with the guy and time goes by, maybe fifteen minutes. And finally, the fellow says, "Gee, I wonder what's keeping Elaine?" Soupy says, "Wait a minute, isn't this Joanne Pinckard's house?" The fellow says, "No, Joanne lives across the street."

So, Soupy went over there late and Joanne was livid.

Soupy was a writer on the staff of the *Parthenon*, the student newspaper, and I was the sports editor. Unfortunately, he was sometimes late getting his copy in. Every time I tried to find him he'd be over at the student union doing one of his standup routines or dancing. I remember one day we had words in the Exchange room, which is where we'd go to take a look at the newspapers from all over the country. I was tired of getting his copy late, so I finally blew up and said, "Dammit, Soupy, you're fired." He said, "You can't fire me. Only Virginia Lee can fire me." Virginia was the faculty advisor of the paper. He was so mad. He was stomping around the room, waving his arms. So I guess you could say that this was the day that I got my first look at White Fang. Of course, after a while everyone cooled off and within ten days he was hired back onto the staff.

Soupy and I also did a radio show together on the campus station. It was a news show that was broadcast once a week from the student union. In those days instead of cutting tape they made kind of a record of it, what I think they used to call an electrical transcription. The show was done in three parts. The first part was the campus news, Soupy had the middle of the show—I had the end of the show—a five-minute sports bit. During his portion, which was a half hour show, Soupy told jokes, and did all sorts of crazy things, and I think he may have played records as well. I could hear it all when it was played on the downtown radio station the next day, which believe me, was quite a thrill.

Through Soupy I was able to audition for a local radio station, but I realized that that wasn't my bag. I do remember that oftentimes, during the handover, when the show was handed over from Soupy to me, I would be so busy laughing at what he'd just done that I could hardly pull myself together. And it didn't even have to be something he said. Mostly, I just cracked up looking at him. At the time he had this facial expression, his face was pulled down and his eyes were looking up, that was just hysterically funny.

I remember a particular incident that occurred at our senior dance, which took place at the Dreamland, a public pool in a town adjacent to Huntington. It was a beautiful spot, built into a hillside, and the pool itself was just enormous. Anyway, at that time West Virginia was a semi-dry state, which meant that you had to pack your own liquor. So, naturally, we had brought our own supply. Well, the band was playing and I remember that the bandleader, whom Soupy knew somehow, would come down during every break and would drink our liquor. Finally, Soupy made some kind of witty, smart remark to him. But we thought it was all pretty funny.

Soupy was always a lot of fun to be around. He seemed to be in perpetual motion, even when he was standing still. He was very polite, but if you gave him the chance he was always "on." He'd be out there in the middle of the floor dancing and telling jokes. But he also had his serious side—we all did. Most of us, having grown up during the Depression, were driven, very ambitious, and Soupy, for all his easygoing attitude, was still a very serious guy. But he was also and still is, a very sensitive, emotional person who attaches a great deal of value to friendships. Whenever he's down here visiting, which used to be three or four times a year, he loves to go down and visit old places. For instance, he'll go over to Eleventh Avenue and stand outside the house where he grew up, but will not go inside. I know for a fact that people who've lived there have invited him in, but he won't go. He wants to remember it the way it was when he lived there.

There's still a group down here that's very close. Now, whenever Soupy comes down we'll have reunions at a restaurant or often at people's houses. The Marshall School of Journalism had a roast for me to raise money for the j-school, which has turned out some very prominent journalists, and Soupy agreed to emcee the roast. He threatened to "burn me at the stake." As I said, he's very sensitive and emotional about his past, so he was anxious to help out, to do something for his old school. We raised twenty thousand dollars for the school, and all Soupy got out of it was a chance to go on the local radio station, which actually meant that he got absolutely nothing for doing it.

. . .

Occasionally, I was inspired to take my antics off the radio airwaves and directly onto campus. One day, on the way to catch a Marshall basketball game, I noticed a dead pigeon lying in the street. Suddenly, an idea occurred to me and I picked it up and put it in my pocket. In those days, there was no buzzer, so at the end of the first half the referee would always fire off a blank pistol, pointed up in the air, toward the rafters. So, that day, when the ref fired his pistol, I lobbed that dead pigeon high into the air. My aim was pretty good, because it eventually fell right at the referee's feet. The ref stared at the dead pigeon, then at his gun, then at the rafters. The crowd went crazy.

Another time, I was in class with the celebrated journalism professor W. Page Pitt—for whom the university has now named a school of journalism and mass communications—when he challenged us to come up with a story in less than an hour about a brutal murder that happened in Milton involving a guy who had butchered his wife with an ax. Pitt handed out an eight-by-ten-inch glossy photo of the murder victim. I remember some girls were practically fainting, others almost throwing up. I took a look at that photo and said simply, "The story's easy. She's got a splitting headache." Pitt glared at me and then shouted, "Get out of here." I guess that was my first bad review.

. . .

Marines build men. Drop us a line and we'll send the parts.
—Phony radio ad from Soupy's show

. . .

By 1943 we were two years into World War II, and I was one semester into college. But I was nearly eighteen and the draft board was breathing down my neck. I figured I'd save them the time and trouble of sending me out a notice, so I went down to the draft board and volunteered. Unfortunately, they told me they already had enough members on the board.

Actually, before the draft caught up to me I enlisted in the Navy, choosing that branch of the service over the Army, primarily because I preferred to have a roof over my head and a reasonably comfortable place to sleep.

When I left Huntington to enter the service, I was still only seventeen years old. In retrospect, I'd have to say that the day I entered the Navy was the day I became a man. At that age I was enthusiastic and awed by life, and the fact that I was getting ready to go into the service didn't faze me in the least. It was the first time I was ever away from home, but I think I adapted to it pretty well, and it turned out to be a great experience. I did my basic training in San Diego, California, where I witnessed a terrible airplane accident that I don't really like to talk about. After our training period was over, I was assigned as a Seaman, First Class, to the U.S.S. *Randall,* flagship of the Seventh Fleet. We served during the invasion of Okinawa, which was surely one of the most frightening experiences of my life—the ferocious shelling and the constant threat of kamikaze attack. I've never before or since heard such an awful, deafening roar or seen such brilliant flashing light in the night sky—maybe it's the burnishing effect of memory, but even the spectacular Macy's-sponsored Fourth of July fireworks display over the East River, which I've watched religiously each year from the terrace of my New York apartment, pales alongside it. No one who has not lived through battle can comprehend the kind of fear that every instant could be your last. In our case, that fear carried over after V-J day, when the fighting was ostensibly at an end. The *Randall* was the ship that delivered the first atomic bomb to the Bikini atoll—and I've always wished that we'd stuck around long enough for me to see it exploded.

After the bombs were dropped on Nagasaki and Hiroshima, and Japan officially surrendered, we were on our way back to the States when we found we were being pursued by a Japanese submarine. I was scared to death. I remember one of the other crewmen said, "Hey, somebody tell those guys the war is over!" But, of course, you couldn't tell those guys anything. To this day, I still sometimes wake up from nightmares about the war.

DAVE USHER, DETROIT FRIEND:

As a result of his experiences during the war, Soupy hated to fly. He told me that when he was in the Navy, either prior to being on ship or perhaps after, he was stationed at a naval air station in San Diego and there was a horrible plane accident and he was part of the detail that had to clean it up. As a result, he had a dreadful nondesire to fly. The first time he flew with me—I think we were going to New York—I had a terrible time trying to convince him to go. I know he used to take pills when he had to fly to get through it.

• • •

In spite of all those wartime terrors, I have many warm memories of the Randall because of the wonderful camaraderie, the bonds of friendship I formed with men of wildly diverse backgrounds. In a sense, we all grew up together, united by that unique shared experience. I still travel to our annual reunions, and more than half a century later, I proudly wear my U.S.S. Randall baseball cap whenever I'm going around the streets of Manhattan, whether it's lunch at the Friars Club, a barber's appointment, or a jazz show at Birdland or the Blue Note.

On the ship, I was the chaplain's assistant—I think three hundred guys changed religion because of me—and I also tried my hand at broadcasting, via the ship's onboard intercom. I had sort of an informal show where I'd play music and tell jokes, do anything to keep the rest of the sailors amused. That's where I first came up with the idea for White Fang. I'd always been a big fan of Jack London, and as a boy I'd always imagined creating the comic character of an intractably unruly dog by the name of White Fang, who I always pictured as being a friend of mine. But the catch was, you couldn't control him—he would just do whatever he wanted to do. One night, I was playing a V-disc of *Hound of the Baskervilles* over the intercom to entertain the whole ship and we reached the point where Sherlock Holmes hears the hound on the moors and there's this incredibly gravelly growl, and immediately I said to myself, "that's White Fang," and I filed it in the back of my mind for future reference. Leaving nothing to chance, I "confiscated" that disc and used it on my intercom show all throughout the rest of my time in the Navy—I'm confessing now because I don't think I have to worry about a court-martial at this point, since I'm sure the statute of limitations has long run out. Besides, the evidence is long gone because years later, when I was working in Detroit, someone stole that disc from *me,* and I had to come up with the voice myself. But that's another story.

One day, the captain of the ship called me over and said, "I've been told that you can put on a show. You can take all the guys you want and take all the time you want, and I want you put on a show for the men next Sunday."

I was thrilled for the opportunity to get out of that cramped intercom room and come up into the fresh air and do my part to entertain the troops, sort of a pint-sized Bob Hope, without the beautiful pinup girls, of course. In enemy waters, you did anything to try to keep up morale, so I worked on my live show all week, wrote the whole thing, put the show together by finding people who could perform. A couple of them were going to sing, some others would tell jokes, while I was going to emcee and do a little standup routine.

Well, the morning of the show came, and when I went looking for the guys, I couldn't find any of them. It was as if they had all fallen off the side of the ship. I was stuck. I couldn't call the show off, because everyone was looking forward to it. So I just went up there myself and launched into a one-man show that lasted an hour and a half. It wasn't so bad, and really, I wasn't very nervous. After all, I had a captive audience because they weren't about to walk out on me unless they were ready to swim to the nearest island. I was standing there on the deck of the ship, with the microphone in my hand, and I just went for it. I think I told every joke I ever knew, and maybe some of them twice. I was writing my own material by this time, and I used stuff that I did about people on the ship. And they loved it. And I loved it, because very early on I was addicted to the drug of applause. It's like somebody has given you a blood transfusion when you needed blood, or somebody's given you the breath of life when you needed a breath. It's just the greatest panacea for any ills that can befall you.

But it certainly didn't go to my head or give me any bigger ideas. In those days, no one would ever say, "Soupy, someday you're going to be a big star." I was just another sailor, the chaplain's assistant, who happened to play records and tell stories over the ship's intercom. And it wasn't as if there were any talent scouts on board, although there was this one guy I met, his name was Johnny Faunce, who to me was the closest thing to a show-business contact. After the war, he became a tennis pro and lived Los Angeles. When I got out of the Navy I wrote him, told him what I wanted to do, and asked him if he knew anyone who could represent me. But he never answered my letter. Maybe he remembered that U.S.S. *Randall* show.

The funny thing is, after that triumphant show, I never did perform before an audience again until I got out of the service, simply because there was never another opportunity to have a show on board.

After two years, my tour of duty was over, and I came back to Huntington and reenrolled in college at Marshall on the GI Bill. I got my job back on the school newspaper and settled into college life.

• • •

Here are some travel tips for those of you who intend to visit Europe or Asia this year. If you're tall and blonde, go to Naples. You'll be a big hit. If you're short, squat and dark, go to Sweden. It will help your ego tremendously. Women will stare at you. And small children will claw at your locks. And while you're at it, try the lox. You want to get beat up? Try Singapore. As for luggage and clothing, by all means, go as you are, with a pair of socks in each pocket. In case of rain, you can slip one over your head, but don't let a nervous old lady see you after sundown.

—Phony Radio Ad

. . .

At the same time I picked up my attempts at higher education, I started to perform some comedy gigs in nearby clubs, most of which were pretty seamy. They were the kinds of places where they played the "Star Spangled Banner" every fifteen minutes just to see who could still stand up. But I didn't care. I was performing . . . and they were actually paying me for it (though not much), and that's all that mattered to me. I remember that the first time I saw my name in lights, so to speak, I was so thrilled that I actually took a picture of it.

In my act, and I use that term very loosely, I'd still use some of the jokes I'd taken from those joke books I'd collected, but I'd also written a lot of my own material. I remember one joke I used to tell: "A couple was on their honeymoon, on their way to the Old Log Inn. The weather was terrible. It was pouring rain. It was cold. Their car breaks down. The husband gets out of the car and starts walking down the deserted road, looking for help. Finally, he sees a guy on the side of the road and he goes up to him and asks, 'How far is the Old Log Inn,' and the guy beats the shit out of him."

Those were rough places, just local roadhouses sometimes, either in West Virginia or Ohio. They'd usually have maybe three acts: a tap dancer, a stripper, a singer, or a comedian. I did a fifteen- or twenty-minute act, and I'd get fifteen bucks a night. There would usually be two shows a night, seven nights a week, so I was doing fourteen shows for about a hundred bucks. And I had to pay my own way out of that princely sum. And then sometimes I'd be booked into talent contests, but I'd never win any of those. It was always some singer who sang, "Love Is Where You Find It" or something like that. Comedy was always the lowest rung on the ladder.

Although the possibility was always there, incredibly enough I didn't bomb very often and I think that's because I always tried to be prepared. Every once in a while I'd really win the crowd over and then, when I did, it was as if I were suddenly able to fly. You see, there's no feeling in the world like the sound of applause and laughter, particularly if it happens to you. Looking back on my grade-school performance of mine as Peter Rabbit, I can understand why I was hooked.

I was pretty good with one-liners, but there was one time that it got me into real trouble. I was working this club, performing my act and acting as kind of an emcee, introducing other acts, and the stripper, a very beautiful girl named Vivian Morgan, took me aside one night and said to me, "Listen, after you're finished doing your fifteen minutes, I want you to come back, and when the guys throw silver dollars onto the stage, you pick 'em up and give 'em to me after the show." I said, "Sure," what do I know? So, while she's doing her strip routine—she was very popular and she used to strip down to a G-string and pasties—people from the audience would be tossing these silver dollars onto the stage, and I'd be there catching them, and sometimes I'd even catch 'em on the first bounce. So, one Saturday night, after I'd done my fifteen minutes, I'm out there picking up the silver dollars, and this guy in the audience, I remember he was a big guy wearing a mackinaw coat, said to Vivian, "Hey, I threw the silver dollar, I want *you* to pick it up." And she said, "No, this kid is working for me." So, while he's talking to her, I'm onstage picking these things up, and all of a sudden he comes right up through the ring. You see, the place used to house boxing matches, so the stage was kind of in the configuration of a boxing ring, and, as a matter of fact, the name of the club was Ringside, primarily because the owner was a big Rocky Marciano fan. Again, he says to Vivian, "I want you to pick them up," and she says, "No, that's his job," pointing to me. And the guy says, "Yeah, well, you're not that great looking. My wife at home has a better-looking body than you do." Without thinking I said, "Okay, then why don't we just go back to your house?" and he hauls off and punches me, and I go down like a rock. Meanwhile, the crowd is laughing hysterically. They think it's all part of the show. Next thing I know, I wake up in the dressing room. When someone asked me about it, I said, "I never even saw it coming."

Since then, I really haven't been heckled very much, but when it does happen, I've found that the best way to handle it is just to go along with the heckler. It's better to be a friend than to be an enemy, so I try to make light of it and make an ally out of him, get him on my side, and in that way avoid a sticky—and in some cases, potentially dangerous—situation.

Another time, I was working this club, and one night I went on and I bombed. I mean, nothing. Nada. Fifteen minutes seemed like fifteen hours. I come backstage and the owner is there, and he says to me, "You're the worst comedian I've ever seen and I'm not gonna pay you." I said, "C'mon . . ." I was really bummed out, but I still had one more show to do that night, so I went out and did it and I killed. I go backstage and there's the owner again, and this time he says to me, "Hey, why don't you stick around for the next couple of days." That's the way it is. One minute you're down in the depths: the next minute you're riding high. It's a good thing to keep in mind, because life is pretty much like that, too.

Frankly, even though I was doing a lot of it, I wasn't particularly crazy about working in front of a live club audience. After all, most of my experience up to that point was in radio, in the studio, and that's what I liked best.

• • •

Those years at Marshall were a special time for me. The area was alive and jumping with great bands at Dreamland Pool, St. Cloud Commons, the Hotel Frederick and the Prichard—performers like Tommy Dorsey, Glenn Miller, the Bernie Theis Band, Howard Jennings and the Guy McComas Band. And Huntington had some of the best eateries—Jean's Swiss Shop had the best hamburgers, Jim's Spaghetti House, the best spaghetti, Stewart's, the best hotdogs, Midway, the best barbeque, Brackman's, the best chili, and the Whirligig had the best waffle-grilled cheese sandwich. Man, those were the days!

In 1949, when I finally graduated from Marshall with that degree in journalism—and I want you to know that not long ago I was

*Ernie Salvatore and my radio show at the Marshall Student Union—
that's Ernie with the glasses, facing me.*

La Jolla, 1944—On shore leave from the Navy.

*Marshall College, 1943—Announcing the College Queen competition.
I was second runner-up.*

given an honorary doctorate's degree from my alma mater, so you can call me Dr. Soupy Sales, and yes, I'm making house calls now— I went looking for a full-time job in radio. There were four radio stations in town. I knocked on the door of WPLH, a 250-watt station, hoping I'd be hired. But the station manager told me that I had to "start small" to which I said, "Hey, there isn't anything smaller than a 250-watt station." He grabbed me and threw me out on the sidewalk. Thank God, I ran into Dean Stern of the somewhat larger rival station, WHTN, whose offices were across the street. I told him what happened and he immediately hired me as a writer for twenty bucks a week. It wasn't long before I, using the name Suppy Supman, became the top-rated deejay in Huntington.

Working at WHTN was quite a training ground. Back then, the job of writer consisted of writing what they called continuity, which meant you wrote the commercials. On Sundays there were a bunch of different fifteen-minute shows featuring singers like Mel Torme or Vic Damone, and I'd write those. I'd also hand copy to the deejay, and I'd write three or four lines and end with some kind of joke. That caught on, and the next thing I knew I was going on the air, too, writing two-man things. So now I was not only doing some writing, but I was also doing some on-air stuff as well.

One day, the regular on-air guy got fired, so I went to the general manager of the station and told him I'd like to go on the air, taking the old guy's place. But he said, "No, we need you to write copy." I said, "I don't want to do that anymore." So, I quit. Well, not long after that the general manager left and was replaced by a fellow named George Brengel. He said he'd hire me back and I could go on the air, but I also had to go out and sell commercials. So, I'd go out and I'd sell spots, which cost the advertisers a buck a piece. I'd sell airtime to gas stations, shoe shops, drug stores—anyplace I could find. Well, selling the spots was the easy part. The hard part was collecting the dough—and they had to pay in cash, no checks, please. I'd wind up spending three days selling air time and four days collecting.

I got the hang of it pretty soon, and it wasn't too long before I was getting three bucks and sometimes more for the spots that I sold. At the same time, I was still doing some writing and performing on my own radio show, called "Wax Works," which was a couple of hours a day. I'd be spinning records, telling jokes, selling time, and writing commercials, and by the time I added up all the money I was making it came to the unheard of amount at the time, especially for someone in his early twenties, of about $250 a week.

In 1950, when I was twenty-four, I was still working at WHTN in Huntington, I was still living with my mother, paying her rent. By this time, my stepfather had died, and I was getting tired of living at home. I figured it was just about time to move out into the world. I was dating a young woman named Barbara Fox—also known as Plaintiff—who was an aspiring singer and model. She was eighteen, had grown up in Huntington—her father worked as a deputy at the courthouse—and she had a good sense of humor, which was certainly a necessity if she was going to get involved with me.

Up until meeting Barbara, I really didn't date much. In fact, most of my love affairs were short, like the time I was driving in a car and I gave this girl the eye and she gave me the eye, and then I gave her a toot on the horn and she gave me a toot on the horn, and that's what it was—an eye for an eye and a toot for a toot.

Like any romance, our relationship went through the usual stages, including the best stage, the one that goes from Kansas to Oklahoma, pulled by four horses (can you hear the drum rolls in the background?). Anyway, after a relatively short courtship, Barbara and I got hitched—but not to a post, I'm afraid.

But little did Barbara know that once we got get married, she'd have to keep her suitcase packed all the time, ready to move at a moment's notice. And that's just what we had to do as my Huntington show got canceled and I realized that if I was going to make it in show business it wasn't going to be in West Virginia.

Cleveland, WJW-AM, 1952. A guy's gotta eat, don't he?

2

SOUPY TAKES THE MIDWEST BY STORM

CINCINNATI—1950, WKRC
CLEVELAND—1951-1953, WXEL

Roses are red,
Violets are blue.
Too many goodies can spoil a meal for you.
And that goes for anything right before dinner.
Cut down on sweets and your appetite will be a winner.
—Soupy's Words of Wisdom

• • •

As luck would have it, one day shortly after my show was canceled, I received a call from George Brengel, the former general manager of WHTN who had been fired and subsequently moved to Cincinnati. "Hey, Soupy," he said, "how'd you like to come to Cincinnati and get into TV?" Frankly, I think he was doing this to spite his old station, but I didn't care. As far as I was concerned, the answer couldn't have been easier: "I'd love it, George."

This was a very exciting prospect for me, to get into TV, which

The Four Aces; Al Alberts, the leader, is third from the left.
The woman kneeling next to me (the Fifth Ace) is Patty Rowe,
my Soup's On *co-star, 1951.*

was really just getting started. Furthermore, the situation couldn't have been better, because I never believed in going somewhere unless you had someplace to go—okay, let me put that another way: I wasn't going to leave a good job and move to another city to find work that I didn't have; and now I didn't have to do that. A job had found me.

And so, now married to Barbara, I picked up and moved to Cincinnati, and took my first professional television gig with WKRC in Cincinnati, which was owned by the illustrious Taft family—as in William Howard Taft, the corpulent twenty-seventh president, and Senator Robert Alphonso Taft, the powerful Mr. Republican, one of the most influential members of Congress.

In those days television was a lot different from what it is today. Mostly, you'd turn on the set and you'd see a lot of snow. It was very, very raw. The sets, if you could even call them that, were primitive. And, because television was in black and white—that's right, no color, gang, just shades of gray—you had to wear lipstick just so your lips would show up on screen. In part, this was because the lights were so strong, they just washed out the features of your face.

I began my Cincinnati career by changing my name, at the station's request, from Suppy Supman to Soupy Hines, after the Hines Soup Company (it was not, despite popular belief, the Heinz company of ketchup fame), which was locally popular at the time. This change has been the source of widespread confusion about my original name, which is still listed in many publications as "Milton Hines."

It was my idea to host a television dance show for teenagers, which was going to be called *Soupy's Soda Shop*. We were going to be on the air every day, Monday through Friday, from 5:30 P.M. to 6:30 P.M. My wife, Barbara, was going to be on the show with me: It would be Soupy and Babs, sort of like the cool, hip chaperones for the school hop, and remember, we weren't much older than the kids who appeared on the show. Barbara was sort of my sidekick, whose job it was to stand there and look pretty, a job I couldn't quite manage on my own. They were going to pay me $180 a week, but that was for both Barbara and me, which wasn't very much money, but it was good enough for me. I wouldn't have told them this even under pain of torture, but I probably would have done it for free.

Although the station wanted a dance show, they left it completely up to me as to what we did with it. But I certainly didn't let this autonomy go to my head. Always, in the back of my mind, there was the sense that if I didn't produce, I was out of there. That's just the way it was, if you didn't do a good job, they'd just go and get somebody else who would.

Not only did I star in the show, but I produced and wrote it as well. Whoever happened to be in town, if they had anything at all to do with music, would be invited onto the show. There wasn't much rock 'n' roll in those days, so what we'd play would be mostly Big Band music, a favorite of mine. I'd also talk to the kids, ask them what school they went to, where they were from, stuff like that. And if we had guests on the show, we'd have a little question-and-answer period, where the kids could talk directly to the celebrity guests. We also used to come up with little quizzes and hand out prizes, anything to keep the viewers and the kids who were dancing entertained. We really had a wild time.

On Tuesday nights a bunch of us would cross over into Kentucky looking for some fun, because Cincinnati had no sin in it in those days, if you get what I mean. On the other hand, Covington, Kentucky, was a wide-open town with plenty of sin to go around. So, we'd go over there and catch Nat King Cole and Georgia Gibbs and then maybe, if we were lucky, we'd have them on our show the next day.

I also started another show, called *Club Nothing*, where I did comedy sketches and interviews, sort of a forerunner of the *Tonight Show*. George Brengel was my sidekick, and he did a little of everything: writing, acting in sketches, and so forth. In a way, I suppose you could say that he was part of my first television repertory company. If I needed somebody for a sketch, George would do it. Anyone who'd come through town promoting one thing or another, we'd get on the show.

After six or eight months of being on the air—and doing pretty well, as far as I was concerned—the Tafts, or rather their flunkies, in their infinite wisdom, informed me that the show had been canceled. As they so wisely put it, "Nobody wants to see a bunch of teenagers dance, so we're canceling the show." So about six months later, a fellow named Dick Clark started *American Bandstand*, and he was on the air for thirty-five years. Go figure. Incidentally, the very same day they fired me, they also cut loose a dark, wiry, intense writer, just a couple of years older than I was, who had a special flair for the macabre. "Get rid of that idiot who writes about people in outer space," they said. That "idiot's" name was Rod Serling, who later went on to develop the classic, *Twilight Zone*. They thought he was just plain nuts. So much for the Tafts and their uncanny programming genius. But what you have to remember is that in those early days of TV, the guys who ran stations were essentially used-car dealers, and the decisions they made had little to do with quality or creativity. The bottom line was the only thing they were concerned with—but then, they weren't alone.

To tell you the truth, when the show was canceled I was pretty devastated, because at the same time they also canceled *Club Nothing* and suddenly I was out of work, and so was my wife because she had been working with me.

The first thing I did after I was canned was to drive to Chicago, because I knew a producer at one of the stations there. But that didn't work out, so I went to a radio station in Cincinnati, WSAI, hoping to land a job there. This was the station where Gene Shepard, who wasn't famous yet, was doing his show, which consisted of him simply sitting around spinning those terrific yarns of his. There were no openings at the station, but someone there knew of a job in Cleveland and he made a call for me, which was very nice of him.

When I spoke to the station's general manager he said, "Come to Cleveland and as soon as you get to town, we want to see you." I think I got there before that guy even had a chance to hang up the phone. Before I checked into a hotel, I parked the car on the street and went to the station for the interview. When I got back, I found that all my clothes had been stolen. The press took a picture of me in my underwear and they ran it in the local newspaper under the headline, "Soupy Hines in his underwear, because everything else he owns has been stolen." A very auspicious beginning, don't you think? Probably scared half the people in Cleveland who were wondering what this idiot wouldn't do to entertain them.

In May of 1951—and by this time, my wife was pregnant with our first son, Tony, who was born on September 26, 1951—I got the job and moved to Cleveland, where I started working as a deejay on radio station WJW. This was a pivotal time for radio in that city. In those days, disc jockeys were playing anything they wanted, which in many cases meant the new music that was beginning to be embraced all over the country. In fact, one of my colleagues was none other than the legendary deejay Alan Freed, who coined the term rock 'n' roll for this revolutionary kind of music—and who, by the way, did his show drunk just about every night. I did a morning show at WJW—one of an incredible eight other morning shows broadcasting from Cleveland—between 6 and 9 A.M., as well as an afternoon show, which meant that the station was obviously getting its money's worth. I was playing music, doing jokes and skits. I would do things like tape radio soap operas and then add my voice to them. I also did a Monday through Friday TV show on WXEL from 11 A.M. to 11:30 A.M., called *Soup's On*. I'd play records and pantomime to them. I'd have on a lot of musical guests, because Cleveland had some great local musical talent, like Johnny Ray. The show really caught on and won awards, and accolades which meant, naturally, that by the end of a year's time it was off the air. To make matters worse, they never even bothered to tell me why.

But something that happened on that show was to change the rest of my life—because that's the first place I introduced pies into my act, and here's how it happened.

Our studio was outside of town, up on a hill, and so often we'd go outside to shoot some bit or another. One day, while we were outside the studio, a local farmer came by and said, "Why don't you use my horse on your show?" I thought, "Why not?" So, I tell the guys, "just get me a loincloth and a feather." At that time, the movie *Broken Arrow*, starring Jimmy Stewart and Jeff Chandler, was very popular, and the name of our sketch was "Son of Broken Arrow," which was going to be, at least I hoped, a funny parody of that movie.

So, I got down there and this farmer had brought one of his horses and the producer said to me, "You've got two minutes, Soupy." Well, first I had to get on the horse and I looked at it and there was something wrong, "Where's the saddle?" I asked. The farmer looked at me like I was nuts and said, "Indians didn't use saddles." I shot

Me, singer Jane Turzy, and my co-host Patty Rowe, Cleveland, 1952.

back, "When did you become the technical advisor for this project?" He countered, "Just get on that horse!"

Now the thing is, when you're young (and desperate) you do things you wouldn't ever do when you're older. But when you're twenty-four, you'd do just about anything—I've got pictures to prove that—especially if you're a comedian and there's the possibility of getting a laugh. So, I get on that horse, and I'm just holding on to its mane (its New Hampshire, and its Rhode Island), and it rides me up the hill and throws me off and yes, the camera is getting all this. So, I'm off the horse and, trouper that I am, I still did my line, "Soldier come to Indian country. You kill our buffalo, you kill our antelope, you shoot our deer, what is left for the Indian?" And, boom, I get hit in the face with a pie from an off-screen hand. And I said, "That's not what I had in mind."

So, that was the first of what I figure has to be at least twenty thousand pies that I've taken in the face. And let me tell you something about the pies we used in those days. First of all, there was no such thing as aerosol shaving cream, so it was either egg whites or whipping cream—that particular first pie was made from egg whites. But we found that you had to be very careful, because if you left the egg-white pies under the lights for too long, the egg whites would separate and so would the whipping cream. But we had to make do with that until aerosol shaving cream came along a year or so later. Also, here's a little advice if you're going to be hit in the face with a pie (like, who hasn't been?). The best thing to do, if you want the laugh, that is, is to just stand there and act as if you haven't the foggiest notion that you're going to be hit with a pie, that it's the last thing in the world you'd expect to happen. Take my advice, and you're bound to get a laugh . . . not to mention a mouth full of shaving cream.

The pie-in-the-face turned out to be an incredibly popular bit, but it was something that I had been thinking of for a while, it's just that the time never seemed right. But now it was and we made good use of it over the years. Just ask Frank and Sammy and Burt and Tony, among many, many others. People have asked me if there's anyone I haven't hit with a pie that I would have liked to, and it's not an easy question to answer. Over the years, I've hit a lot of people, people with big names, and they've all been great sports about it.

But the real coup would be to hit someone who has a lot of dignity—someone like Henry Kissinger, maybe—because then you'd really get the laugh. And that's what it's all about, isn't it?

My ongoing fight with WJW was with the program director Bruce MacDonald, who became program director after I took over the morning show that he had hosted, and the fights were something like this: I'd come in one morning, and he'd complain that I was talking too much—not enough music. So another morning I'd come in and he'd say, "Too much music—not enough talk." It went on like this for several weeks. It was obvious he was jealous because I had made a sucess of the morning show, taking it from eighth place into first place. After he chewed me out one day, I said, Bruce, make up your mind. What do you want me to do?" He said, "Why don't you quit?" So I said, "Have my check waiting for me at the end of the day," because I realized that once you're put on the spot like that, you've got to make a move because it becomes a no-win situation.

And so, after two years in Cleveland, it was time to move on to what I hoped would be greener pastures. But although I didn't know it then, the best was yet to come.

Detroit, 1955.

3

Soupy Sweeps into Motown

Detroit—1953–1959, WXYZ

*He broke ground. He set a trend. He was an original. Everything
we did was new. Everything we did was great. Everything we did
was groundbreaking. It was fun. Most television programming
in those days was radio shows converted to television, like game
shows. But here was a unique guy in radio, with a great sense of
humor and timing. There'll never be anyone else like him.*
      —Bill Carruthers, director of *Lunch with Soupy*

• • •

Finding work in either radio or television wasn't easy and so, with
several mouths to feed—not mine, I've got only one, but those of
my family—I decided the only thing to do was to go back to my
roots: standup comedy, which meant going on the road again. I
remember in those days I spent most of my time on the phone, trying to line up work. But because I didn't want to be away from my
family for too long, I would take only those gigs that were within
driving distance of Cleveland—places like Erie, Pennsylvania, and

Mansfield, Ohio. I'd get fifty bucks a night, and out of that I had to pay my own expenses, which didn't leave me with much. But at least it was something.

I was doing most of my own material—I wish I had a record somewhere of what I did, but the routines were never written down, they were just performed—and when I felt they got tired, I just retired them to the old joke home and wrote some more. Usually I was on the bill with a singer and a strip act, which might sometimes be a belly dancer. The clubs were small, and I would often double as an emcee. Because I had something of a reputation, the audiences, for the most part, were receptive and so it was fun. But it also had its horrible side because I was working by myself, with no safety net, no security. In short, this was a very tough time for me because I never knew what I was going to be doing from day to day, and the uncertainty was wearing on me.

This was the life I lived for six or seven months until 1953, when a friend, Stan Dale, who had moved from Cleveland to Detroit, advised me that I ought to look for work there because he was convinced it would be a good place for someone of my talents.

So I hopped into my car and drove to Detroit, where I tried three stations before I finally wound up at the television station WXYZ. As it happened, John Pival, who was head of the station and a true programming genius, had seen me in Cincinnati, but I didn't know that till later. I talked to some of the executives at the station, and when I got back to Cleveland I received a phone call asking, "Will you come up and audition?" So, that's what I did. I brought some sound effects, including my trusty (hot) White Fang recording. I'm not sure what I actually did for the audition, but it was pretty wild. Not that I was nervous. If you're prepared, you're not very nervous. Actually, once they asked me to audition, I was pretty confident that I'd get the job. And when I did my thing, everybody laughed, which was great. The crew seemed to be very good and they seemed to like me (translation: they laughed at my jokes.) Funny thing is, while I was auditioning I thought it was just a run-through, a rehearsal, but when I finished, they said, "Okay, you'll hear from us," which meant they were considering it the real thing.

I returned to Cleveland and went back on the road again. A few days later, I got a phone call from the wise folks at WXYX and I was told, "We want you to work for us—a hundred and sixty bucks, five shows a week." I said, "Make it two hundred." They said, "Okay."

And that's how I motored into the Motor City.

Detroit turned out to be my Mecca, the place where I established and nurtured my career. It's also where I changed my name for the last time (at least I hope it was for the last time). Now my "Soupy Hines" monicker was working against me—apparently, it reminded people too much of Heinz, the ketchup company, and as a result none of the other food products would buy air time. So, for a long time, while they tried to think up a name for me, I was known only as "Soupy." Station promos would say, "Stay tuned, Soupy's on." People would call in and ask, "What's his name?" and they'd say, "We don't know." One day, in 1957, John Pival, who was running the station, took me aside and said, "Chick Sales was a great old comic, how about 'Soupy Sales'?" Actually, he meant Chick Sale, singular, an actor of the early talkies who made a specialty of playing grizzled old men—even though he was only fifty-one when he died in 1936. So, Soupy Sales was born (or hatched) and several years later I changed it legally from Milton Supman after my kids' school called up my wife and asked why Tony and Hunt hadn't shown up in class for weeks. This came as a shock to us, since as far as we knew they'd been going every day. It turned out that when the teacher took attendance and called out "Supman," Tony and Hunt weren't answering because they thought their name was Sales.

• • •

He set a trend in television for comedy along with Steve Allen and Ernie Kovacs. I think he belongs in that league.
—Bill Carruthers

• • •

John Pival wanted a show where I'd have lunch with the kids every day. I didn't have any experience working with kids (remember, those "kids" in Cincinnati were teenagers) but then again, there weren't actually going to be any kids on the show, just watching it. *Lunch with Soupy Sales* was the name we came up with. The only thing the station originated was the costume: it was their idea for me to wear a ridiculous top hat, an oversized bow tie, and a black sweater. Everything else on the show was what I came up with: White Fang and then later Black Tooth, Pookie, and Hippy were all developed by me.

As far as the costume was concerned, in those days when you were looking for a job, you didn't care what they wanted you to wear. If you wore a top hat, a bow tie, or anything else funny, it was automatically a "kid's show." But there was a funny thing about that costume. I remember something that happened years afterwards, when I was doing the show in California. I had my own dressing room, but I shared the bathroom and shower with the guy who did a clown show there in the morning, Koko the clown, or something like that. He had just finished taping when I would come in. I'd talk with him while he took a shower, and it was always fascinating to watch. It was like seeing a Sherwin Williams paint sign come to life. Clowns wear something like eight different colors of makeup, and when he took a shower the colors would just stream down his body. I found that fascinating and one day he asked me what the big attraction was. "Well," I said, "it's the idea that you take all that time putting on the makeup and then you get in the shower and the colors all run down your drain. Your character runs down the drain."

"Yeah," he said, "but the difference is the people know me as the clown. When I take off this makeup I can go to a bar, pick up a girl, and I can get drunk and nobody knows it's me! But if you do it, they know it's you."

"Yeah," I replied, "but when you want to go in for a raise, they say, 'Nuts to you. We'll pick somebody else up.' Do you think Ronald McDonald gets a raise? They say, 'Nuts to you! Bring in another guy!'

Well, the guy hadn't ever thought about that and it blew him away. He was never the same because he was always afraid that if he asked for something they were going to get rid of him. And you know what, eventually they did.

· · ·

We were a kid's show, but our biggest audience was adults.
—Frank Nastasi, actor

Me and Pookie in Detroit.

The show was raw, but it was very creative. We went on at 12 noon, because that's when the kids were supposed to have come home from school for lunch. At the end of each show I'd create the menu for the next day. For instance, I'd say, "Tomorrow, we're going to have peanut-butter-and-jelly sandwiches, with a big glass of milk, kids." And to this day, I'm sure that those kids went to their parents after the show was over and handed them a menu for the next day's lunch. I guess, over the years, I was responsible for shaping the eating habits of thousands of Detroit kids.

• • •

When I watch some of the few shows that we have on tape, I'm amazed. I say, we did that? I can't believe it. And we did it with a fifty-cent budget.

—Bill Carruthers

• • •

When I started doing the show on WXYZ in 1953, it was in front of a plain flat, that is, just a cardboard backdrop painted to look like the wall of a clubhouse. But there's only so much you can do in front of something that doesn't open or slide or that you can have access to. Finally, I said that I'd like to have a door—because that meant I could have visitors come to the door, which would allow me to do all kinds of bits, like this one:

There would be a knock at the door. I'd answer it. The audience wouldn't see anything but a gesturing hand. For instance, a voice (we never actually saw who was at the door) would be selling me something. I'd say, "Okay, I'll buy it," and I'd take it from him.

"Wait a minute, buddy, that'll be fifty cents," the voice would say.

"Fifty cents?"

"Yeah."

"I have a dollar here," I'd say, and I'd hand it to him. "Gee, thanks, buddy, see you."

"Wait a minute, I gave you a dollar. I have half a buck coming back."

And then there'd be a big, old deer's head handed to me.

But more importantly, having a door also allowed for a hand to come in through it and hit me with, you guessed it, a pie.

After they gave me a door, I wanted to push the envelope a little further. I said, "Well, now let's get a window"—that way I could have Pookie come to the window, allowing me to do bits with him. Originally, Pookie, the lion, was modeled after an old Bil Baird puppet, Charlemagne. I fell in love with that puppet, but of course I couldn't use it, because it was Baird's property. At first I took all the hair off the puppet and called it "Pookie" after the nickname I called my son, Tony. A little while later, it must have been around 1954, I guess, I designed another version of Pookie, and a friend of mine recommended an artist who lived in Greenwich Village who might be able to create him for me. It cost me five hundred dollars, and although that was a lot of money in those days, it was money well spent. At first, Pookie's voice was only a whistle, which Clyde Adler, an engineer and Floor Director at the station, would do. Later, when Frank Nastasi took over Clyde's role, first when Clyde went on vacation and then when he decided he no longer wanted to be an actor on the show, Pookie actually developed a voice.

Once we introduced Pookie as a regular character, we developed what we called the Pookie Players and did bits like this:

In the background, the song, *Fairytales Can Come True*, is playing and I'm reading from a book of fairytales:

"Little Bo-Peep has lost her sheep and doesn't know where to find them," and Pookie, who was really a bit of a hipster, says in a very condescending tone of voice, "Well, that's reasonable, isn't it? It's reasonable to assume if Little Bo Peep has lost her sheep, it's only natural that she wouldn't know where to find them."

Incidentally, it was in my early days in Detroit that somebody stole that *Hound of the Baskervilles* record—I have no idea who it was. Maybe someone from the U.S.S. *Randall* on a special mission sneaked into Detroit one night and . . . But in a way, it turned out to be a very fortunate theft, because it was at this point that White Fang really came alive. One of the engineers' wives had made a hairy glove for Clyde to use, so White Fang could now actually "appear" on TV (even though only his "paw" was visible and the rest of him was left to the imagination), and at pretty much the same time Clyde started ad-libbing a voice for "the meanest dog in the world." I thought this was really great because he could do much more with the character.

Later, we added a phone to the set, so I could field fake calls. And then came a radio, so I could tune in for the weather report and, instead, get all kinds of zany announcements, soap operas, bogus ads, and silly little bits, like:

A woman's voice: "Help! Help!"
Radio announcer's voice: "Ladies and gentlemen, you have just heard the first robin of spring."

. . .

Nut-at-the-Door: "What would you do if you were in my shoes?"
Soupy, looking down, making a funny face: "I'd polish 'em."
Boom, Soupy gets hit with a pie.

. . .

The set was supposed to be a representation of my house, kind of like Soupy's clubhouse, and I would be sitting at a table with a checkered tablecloth and I'd be having lunch. I'd say, "Today, we're having a glass of juice," and then there'd be a sound effect of the juice pouring ". . . and a glass of milk," and you'd hear the pouring of the milk, " . . . and a hotdog . . . " Then, White Fang would come in and visit me during lunch and we'd do some kind of bit.

There were a whole lot of ad-libs out there for me and there were no writers, except for me. Hell, there wasn't any money for writers, so the show was dependent totally on me to be entertaining and funny. Which brings up an age-old question: What is comedy? Or better yet, what's funny? Well, if I had to give you a short answer, it would probably be this: If a person falls down and he doesn't get up, it isn't funny, but if a person falls down and he gets up, it is funny.

The main thing that the station wanted at the beginning was for me to have lunch with the kids, but I never sat down and said, "Well, a seven-year-old kid will like this and an older person will like that." I just set out to do the funniest show I could. See, I don't believe comedy can be done by committee. I would write the show, but if anybody came up with a better line or a better situation when we talked it over—great! Of course, there was never any real rehearsal. We never had any time for that. Back in those days the networks didn't even start broadcasting until four or five o'clock in the afternoon, so all the other live shows, like *The Mickey Mouse Club*, which was ABC's first show of the afternoon, didn't start until four o'clock. And all the other shows, all around the country, whether it was Detroit or Cincinnati or Pittsburgh, were all live, local programs. The closest thing we have to a live show today is the news—or maybe *Saturday Night Live*, but remember, even with the *SNL* show they have a *live* rehearsal, with an audience, right before going on nationally, so by the time it gets on the air, it's pretty well locked in.

Our shows were not actually written, but they were precisely thought out until the point where we knew when we had to get into a commercial. But the greatest thing about the show, and I think the reason for its success, was that it *seemed* undisciplined. When you get right down to it, though, it was *extremely* disciplined. The more you can make a performance *seem* spontaneous, the better the entertainer you are. But that also probably hurt me all through my career, because in this business you get typecast very quickly. It wasn't long before they were saying, "Well, the only thing he can do is get hit with a pie and, look out, he's wild! You don't know what the hell's going on. You don't know what's going to happen." Well, *we* always knew. But that was the idea: to make it *seem* undisciplined. People watched every day precisely for that reason: because they never knew what was going to happen.

And, believe me, unexpected things did happen. I remember one time we were working with Pookie at the window. He was doing a bit where he was breaking eggs and one of the eggs turned out to be rotten. Boy, did he stink up the place. My God, the smell was terrible! And I'm sure, watching us at home, everyone knew there was something wrong from the look on our faces.

• • •

So, here we had this television show, but we had this imagery of two huge dogs, represented by two paws that came into range of the black-and-white camera from the left and the right frame, with these two very distinct voices.

—Bill Carruthers

• • •

Doing a daily show like we did wasn't easy. Remember, I had to kill a half hour of air time every day and I was out there pretty much by myself. Sometimes, we'd show a film and I'd narrate it, adding funny commentary. Sometimes I'd just put on some music and do funny dances, most of them improvised. I was like a traffic cop out there. And the theme that ran through the show was that I could never win. I was always put upon. I think in part, that's why the viewers connected with me. I was one of them. I was the little guy who was sometimes overwhelmed with life, but who somehow always managed to get through it. It was a lot of pressure, because I knew that if I didn't do a good job, then they'd just get somebody else to take my place.

But slowly, the show began to grow. I was getting new ideas. I was adding characters—for instance, after about a year of being on the air, a friend of mine said, "White Fang is so big, maybe you should have a counterpart, a sweet dog." So, I developed Black Tooth, the sweetest dog in the whole wide world. Clyde—who was like a partner on the show, but who was never seen by anyone—worked both White Fang and Black Tooth, who, unlike White Fang who did everything he could to bug me, was always kissing me and slobbering over me. It turned out to be a brilliant suggestion, because now we both dogs could play against each other. Later, we added Hippy, who didn't talk and was modeled after the great Harpo Marx. And eventually we added Peaches, the Girl Next Door, who wanted to marry me. I played Peaches, wearing a big old wig, and, as I used to say, "Give me a dress and high heels and you can take me anywhere."

· · ·

The audience for the show was basically the crew, and Soupy related to the crew. We had guys behind camera laughing. Stage hands, that was our audience—and that's the greatest audience you can have. Make them laugh, and you've really got something. He never knew what we were going to do and we never knew what he was going to do. It was kind of a challenge thing.

—Bill Carruthers

· · ·

We all got along great. The crew was part of the show. They even got fan mail.

—Frank Nastasi

• • •

Within a month, the show was hot—probably because nobody had ever done anything so ridiculous with pies and water guns before—and it wasn't just the kids who were watching. Locally, we were beating out some of the network staples like *Arthur Godfrey Time* and *The Tennessee Ernie Ford Show* in the ratings. So, I'm sure some of the adults who were watching instead of drinking orange juice and milk with me, were probably downing martinis, at twelve o'clock in the afternoon, wasted out of their minds. Of course, this didn't surprise me—about adults watching, not about drinking martinis—because I knew that my kind of humor appealed to adults and to kids. I never talked down to the kids; I interacted with them the same way I would interact with adults. After all, I was nothing more than a king-sized kid myself. And I think the kids understood and really dug that. But once I found out that adults were watching, too, I never consciously changed anything to play to them. I knew that wouldn't have worked. I just went out there and did the same show.

Another thing that I think added to my popularity is that I broke the "fourth wall" (what we mean by this is that I was acknowledging the existence of an actual TV audience, thereby breaking the "wall" between us) by talking directly to the audience, and I achieved a kind of intimacy by speaking with my face right up to the camera. Nobody worked as close to the camera as I did. I wanted it to seem as if I were right in the room with them, that I really was part of their family.

The way the show behind the scenes worked was like this. In the morning, we'd meet—me and the producer and either Clyde Adler or Frank Nastasi, depending upon who was working with me—and we'd talk about what we were going to do for the show that day. I was pretty much writing the whole show, but things were so loose that everyone had the green light to ad-lib and I'd just have to handle it. So, in effect, we had this blueprint for the show, but it's not as if everything was completely scripted out. But after awhile, because of the commercials, I realized we had to be a little more controlled in terms of the structure of the show.

FRANK NASTASI:

The first time I met Soupy was back in Detroit around 1954, six months to a year after he got there. He was doing the children's television show, *Lunch With Soupy*—and I think by that time he was also doing his late night show, *Soupy's On*. At the time, I was a very popular actor in Detroit and I was working on an eight o'clock morning children's show called *Wixy Wonderland*, named after the call letters of our station, WXYZ-TV. It was kind of an educational show, but we did a little bit of everything—comedy, singing, dancing. In fact, we were a pretty popular show and we lasted four years, which wasn't bad, because at that time they were so cheap about programs. They called it the Golden Age of television, but they didn't know that.

Anyway, we were a pretty popular station, the home of shows like *The Lone Ranger* and *The Green Hornet*.

As I said, we were on before Soupy's show but somebody told me about him and I was curious to find out more about this guy who was supposed to be so funny. I started watching his show and, I was told, he was watching mine. So, one day I went onto the set to watch him work and after the show he said to me, "Frank, I'd like to have you on my show."

I said, "Well, Soupy, you already have a guy—Clyde Adler," God rest his soul. Clyde was a wonderful man who did all the voices—White Fang, Black Tooth, and anything else Soupy needed.

He said, "Well, that's all right. You're not going to be replacing him. But sometimes he goes on vacation and I'd like you to take over."

I said, "Well, I haven't done a lot of your stuff."

And he said, "Don't worry, you could do it, Frank."

I thought about it a minute and then I said, "Yeah, okay. Sure."

I remember the first time I was on his show. We were trying to do a promo where we had Pookie, the little lion who you didn't really think of as a roaring lion, and we were trying to find a voice for him. We didn't like the first voice we had for Pookie, which was kind of an Italian accent; it just didn't work. We tried all kinds of voices and then after I

My first anniversary in Detroit, 1954. Can I eat the whole thing?

got on the show, we still couldn't find a voice for Pookie. Then, one day we were doing The Pookie Players—Pookie was an artist, you know. He was the cutest little lion you ever saw, and he was really very hip. He'd refer to Soupy as "booby." Pookie had to play a lot of the characters in his own plays. So I did one of the characters with a hip, laid-back kind of voice and it struck me—this should be the voice of Pookie. So, I ran out during the break, with the intention of telling Soupy that, but before I could say a word Soupy said, "You got it! That's Pookie!" So now we had a voice for Pookie that actually fit the character.

I didn't only do voices for the show. I was on camera even from the very beginning when we did the talking pictures bit. We would open up on the studio, with pictures on the wall, and I'd come walking in making noise—"Do-do-do dooo. Doo-doo." Anything to make a lot of commotion—or I'd open a door, come in, and I would look at the pictures and then suddenly the pictures would come to life. Sometimes they'd throw things at me.

I was also what they used to call the "nut at the door," because I played many characters that would show up behind the door. I'd get splashed with water. Once in a while, I'd get hit with a pie. But not as much as Soupy. Soupy got it. And he took it. And he never complained about it. *Pow!* He was a very good sport about it.

In the beginning, in the mid-1950s, I was on only when Clyde went on vacation, but eventually I replaced him. I also used to do Soupy's night show. It was a lot like the old Broadway Open House show. I performed in whatever sketches we did. I was a part of the sketch. In a way, I suppose, I was part of Soupy's repertory on both his shows.

We did a lot of sketches that were classics—everybody knew the jokes. It was just like the old days of Old Vaudeville. We'd do gangster bits. We'd do parodies of the movies that were out. We'd do just about anything.

So, Soupy was doing both shows and I was appearing on both shows, but I still wasn't a regular—I was just filling in for Clyde when they needed me, or appearing when they needed another actor. I believe I became a regular because at a certain point Clyde wanted out. I think he wanted to go to the coast or something like that. So, Soupy approached me and said, "Frank, how'd you like to become a regular on the show?" And I said, "Yeah. Why not?"

White Fang was my favorite character because of the freedom I had with him, even though he just grunted. Now something many people don't know is that when Clyde was doing the voice of White Fang, he had a much deeper voice than I did. But, I had a voice that you could identify with more. He'd go, "Ah wuh wuh . . ." I'd go, "Weh, weheh." You see, my voice was more modulated. But I couldn't just grunt. Soupy wouldn't let me get away with that. He said, "you've got to express yourself so we know what you mean," so I used to break him up, because I was a method dog. Soupy would say about my rendition of White Fang, "I understand what he's saying." You see, I was trying to make it more than just grunts, I was trying to kind of put a language to it. But Soupy, who knew what he wanted and knew what was best, would always say, "Don't stray too far away from the dog, Frank. We want that element of fairy land."

So, when Clyde left I was the one doing White Fang, Black Tooth, Pookie, Hippy, Nut-at-the-Door, well, I guess you could say the only thing I wasn't doing was Soupy.

I remember sometimes things didn't go exactly as we planned. One day, I knock on the door and Soupy answers and I'm supposed to be selling antiques. I say to him, "This vase here is worth a thousand dollars. And I can take this thousand-dollar vase and I can put it in this bag and I can smash it on the floor. And it won't break."

And Soupy just goes, "Ahhh,"—with that face of his, "All right, let's see you do it."

Now, I was standing in the doorway, so the audience can see me, and I put the vase in the bag and I raise the sack over my head like I'm going to bring it down and smash it on the floor, but as the thing reaches the top it hits the door jam, and it comes bouncing back and *pow!* It hits me right in the head. And Soupy, who saw this big egg forming on my head, didn't know whether to laugh or go blind.

Of course, things like that would happen all the time. Once, Soupy and I were doing a big fight scene. Soupy had a dummy that looked just like him, with the costume and everything. We were doing so many crazy things, that we were just exhausted. We fell on the floor from laughing. We used to break up on the show. And that was part of the charm of the show. It looked like a rehearsal. It didn't look like a show. Because what kind of a script did we have? We had punch lines. That's all we had.

The way it usually worked was like this: We had a short meeting before the show. Soupy would say, "All right Frank, you do this and you do this." I'll take this punch line and you take that punch line." And that was it. We ad-libbed and filled in all around the punch lines. Sometimes, we would take a three-minute bit and make twenty minutes out of it. That was the wonder of it.

Many times, when we had guest comics come on, they'd say, "OK, where's the script?"

And we'd say, "There's no script."

When I watch the tapes that I have, I'm absolutely amazed. I still can't believe we did that.

Some of the comics we had on in those early days were Fat Jack Leonard, Jack Carter, Jackie Vernon—all the Jacks. And we had the Supremes on before Ed Sullivan did. And yes, he was mad about that, because he thought he had the exclusivity.

Soupy was in Detroit seven years, from 1953 to 1959, but I wasn't there with him the whole time. I left to move to New York. Remember, I was an actor, and at the time, I was doing a play at the wonderful Tent theater in Detroit. The director was hired to do a version of *Mr. Roberts* in New York (the original version, starring Henry Fonda and David Wayne, had played 1,157 performances in 1947–48) and he asked me if I wanted to go with him, and, of course, I said, "Sure." I wasn't going to miss an opportunity like that. Of course later, when Soupy took his show to New York in the mid-sixties, I was still living and working in New York as an actor. When he asked me to, I came back on the show.

My general impression of working with Soupy in Detroit was that it was a joy. He is a very easygoing man. Very hard worker. Very ambitious. And he was very conscientious about his show. If the props weren't right—the crew loved us—but if they goofed, we let them know, but in a nice way.

The show was lunchtime. We usually tried to meet in the office in the morning, before the show, and go over ideas. It was me and Soupy and the producer, Art Seidel, who were at these meetings, and the director of the show, Al Kassell. I liked Art very much. He was sharp. I might say, "Hey, I've got an idea. We'll do this. You do that. I'll do that." I'm sorry to say, Art died not long ago.

We were really good at improvisation. Sometimes Soupy would say an unexpected line to me and even if I didn't know exactly what he wanted,

I could figure it out, primarily because we knew each other so well. Or, if I couldn't figure out what he wanted, I somewhere came up with something that fit. And Soupy did the same. Yes, all of us on that show had to be quick on our feet. You didn't tape it again, it was just there.

• • •

Sad to say, there aren't any tapes around of those *Lunch with Soupy* shows. I was on the air for two years for Jell-O on the ABC network on Saturdays, and practically none of those tapes exist either—I do have one from 1957, which was the original pilot, but that's it. As a matter of fact, of the approximately 350 black-and-white *Soupy Sales* shows we did in New York between 1964 to 1966, we've got only about 75 intact. The station erased all the others. In those days, they always did that, and I wasn't the only one who fell victim to that practice. Stations had no idea what they had. They had no sense that television was part of history, that it played such an important part in the culture of America. It was the farthest thing from their minds that anything could be classic or would be worth saving. "Let's erase 'em and use the tape again"—that was their attitude. It's a damn shame. And when they do "find" old kinescopes or tapes of these shows, like the lost Honeymooners episodes they located several years ago, it becomes a major event. Thank goodness we've got the Museum of Television and Radio in New York now, which has become a repository for many classic television shows.

SOUPY'S WORDS OF WISDOM

People who eat sweets take up two seats.

LARRY STORCH, COMEDIAN, PLAYED AGARN ON "F-TROOP":

It was sometime in the mid-1950s and I was appearing at a little club somewhere outside of Detroit. I was doing my act and someone told me that a local TV personality named Soupy Sales was in the audience. I didn't know Soupy at the time, but I thought that since he was on local TV the audience might like to know he was in the audience, so I might as well introduce him. "Oh, ladies and gentlemen," I said, "there's a guy named Soupy Sales in the audience who you might know and he's sitting right over there. Let's say hello." Well, everyone in the place got up and, in the middle of my show, stormed over to his table. There must have been about two or three hundred people. They mobbed Soupy and there was nobody left for me to play to. It was embarrassing. They left the joint empty.

• • •

The kids in Detroit loved us so much we even started a Soupy Sales fan club and the members were called Birdbaths. I was once asked how I came up with that name, and I replied, "It just happened to grab my fancy, and anybody grabs my fancy better watch out." In truth, I don't know what the hell I was thinking about. But we actually gave out cards to members, and if you still have one of them, I bet it's got to be worth a good fifty bucks or more.

SOUPY SEZ

Show me a toilet in a castle and I'll show you a royal flush.

• • •

It was good TV, exciting TV. This was Soupy's town. He owned it lock stock and barrel. I think the town literally stopped, at least the kids stopped, for Lunch with Soupy. We were all good Birdbaths and we did what we were supposed to do. We watched those Words of Wisdom and we did like Soupy said.

—Erik Smith, news anchor, WXYZ

Soupy grabbed an audience of the very young, their moms and dads and teens. That's almost impossible to do. He became everybody's "guy."

—Dick Clark

• • •

a FaN'S SOUPY MEMORY

Remember "The Pookie Players"? There would be a big fanfare, and Pookie would have an easel, and flip its pages along as the "play" progressed. Usually Hippy would be involved, wearing some ridiculous-looking wig. If Pookie was going to perform a fairy tale, the skit would always begin with Pookie singing the Sinatra theme "Fairy tales can come true, it can happen to you, if you're young at heart . . . "

Whenever Soupy wanted to read something to Pookie, Pookie would try to get comfortable by pulling at Soupy's sweater and pull it all over the place until his head was comfortable on Soupy's shoulder. And could Pookie ever dance! And when he and Soupy had a pie fight, it was a riot—Pookie would get creamed by a pie, and his face would be scrunched up, and he would just slowly stare at the camera and gradually unscrunch his face full of pie. It's so much fun to remember Pookie.

Soupy would read the "Words of Wisdom" and then say, "And now, what do we mean by that?" and a voice off-camera would echo, "Yeah, what do we mean by that?" And after explaining what the words meant, and what you should do instead (because there was always a real-life lesson to be learned), Soupy would look at you and say, "You do dat, I love you and give you a big kiss."

White Fang would always seem to have a roll of dollar bills, or whatever, and Soupy would always look to the camera and ask, "Now where does he get that money?"

The knocks at the door always left you wondering what kind of ridiculous situation would arise. When Soupy opened the door it seemed like you always saw the same 3 or 4 old film shots, like a guy leading an elephant on railroad tracks, a little boy running and falling, or the eyes of Count Dracula, or something like that.

· · ·

DaVE USHER, PERSONAL MANAGER

At the time I met Soupy, in 1953, I was about twenty-three years old and I'd been involved in a record company with Dizzy Gillespie. The record label was DeeGee, for the initials of Dizzy's name. We had just ceased operations and I had gone back to work in the family business, which was oil reclamation. A friend of mine named Bob Carrington worked over at WXYZ, Channel 7, which was an ABC affiliate, and he suggested that I meet Soupy because he thought we'd have a lot in common and that we'd get along pretty well.

So I went down to the station and met him one afternoon, right after his show, *Lunch with Soupy*. We started talking and it turned out he'd been a real avid fan of some of the music that I'd produced on our label. We were talking about this and that music and suddenly he said, "Oh, 3600, that was a really good recording. I liked it very much." Well, I was shocked. The only people referring to numbers when they were talking about records would be a distributor to a manufacturer. Usually, people referred to albums either by the title, the artist, or by the author of tune. I was fascinated by how he thought about it that way. I found out later that prior to doing his show he'd been a disc jockey. But still, to have that kind of memory was astounding to me. And he didn't say anything about having a photographic memory, which I don't think he has. I was fascinated by the way he thought.

Anyway, we found ourselves compatible and we became very good friends. Jazz was our main medium, what we had in common.

At the time I met Soupy, I was dating the young lady who became my wife. Soupy and his wife Barbara and my girlfriend, who was an airline stewardess, and I used to go out together a good many times. In fact, when we decided to get married I asked Soupy to be my best man and my wife asked Barbara to be her maid of honor. Well, we went down to the local courthouse to get married. And we were standing there while the ceremony was being performed and, when they finally pronounced us husband and wife, I was so flustered that I turned around and Soupy and I kissed each other.

As we left the building, which was an old county building, we heard a roar. We looked around and saw that it was coming from a crowd of people. They were chanting, "Soupy, Soupy, Soupy." Evidently, word had gotten out that he was going to be at the courthouse. I remember we walked around toward the parking lot, and looking up to the buildings around us we could see people standing in the windows—they had high windows in those days—yelling "Hi, Soupy." That's how popular he was.

Soupy knew what I was doing with my dad's company and he also knew my background, so one day he said to me, "Dave, why don't you do some personal appearance management for me. It would help me out a lot."

I thought about it and said, "Fine." It was an opportunity to stay around the business. So I handled Soupy's personal appearances. And you have to remember, in those days he would average about five or six calls a day from viewers asking, mainly because of his kids show, if he'd make appearances at various locations.

So, we'd show up wherever and Soupy would dress up in the garb he wore on the show, the high hat and his oversized polka-dot-red-and-white bow tie and a sweater and a shirt—that was his costume.

I remember one particular time when we had a doctor who asked if we'd appear in a suburban community, I believe it was Oak Park, Michigan, for a children's show. We couldn't believe it when we heard his name, which was Dr. Smelsey (pronounced "Smell-see"), and he was, I swear this is true, a foot doctor. Naturally, Soup and I found this very funny.

It was a Friday evening and we had our wives with us because we were going to go out to dinner afterward. We were waiting backstage for the show to go on. In those days, unlike today where the flash is built into the camera, they had flashbulbs that they inserted into the camera. You'd wet your finger, touch the base of the flashbulb, then stick it into the socket to make contact. Anyway, Soup and I were playing with these flashbulbs and the doctor, who was standing close by, had a very nervous reaction. He walked over to us and, very seriously, explained, "I had a real bad case where a fellow stepped on one of these flashbulbs and the pieces went right through his foot." I don't know why, probably because of the doctor's name and his profession, but this broke Soupy and me up.

There was also the time we were on our way to a town called Adrian for a personal appearance; Soup was driving and I was sleeping. At one point—it must have been around midnight—we had to stop for gas and when we did, Soupy went into the restaurant/gas station. And when he came out he was in hysterics. When something was funny to Soupy, he just broke up and that's what was happening. Now in those days, Coca-Cola had those very small bottles. Unbeknownst to us, they were trying out the larger bottles in that area and when Soupy went into the road-house part of the gas station he'd seen one of these large bottles and for some reason this just struck him as hilarious. This was just an example of how Soupy's sense of humor worked. He was very observant and very quick and his humor came from his surroundings. This is why he was able to think on his feet so well. His mind was always working, always looking for the humor in things.

The thing kids really flipped over was they *loved* to do the Soupy shuffle, which was this silly little dance he used to do. These kids would be in hysterics. Many times when we'd go for personal appearances, we'd really need a police escort. It's hard to believe, but Soupy was more recognizable than President Eisenhower. He also had this kind of recognition with adults, because of his evening show at eleven o'clock which would usually beat out his competition, which was the news shows.

What he would do was his cohorts—Pete Strand was one of them—would write the evening show after lunch, and then they would give the lines to the actors who would be in whatever sketch they were doing. Now I would notice something absolutely amazing when I'd watch the show. It was hardly discernible, but Soup would actually lip sync the lines before the other actors would do them. You could see him "saying" the lines and then the actors would say them. He actually knew all their lines and in some part that's probably what his timing success was due to. I related that back to how he knew the record numbers. It fascinated me, because he and I never talked about it.

• • •

There's a knock at the door and a traveling psychiatrist arrives in answer to Soupy's desperate telephone plea for help.
Soupy: Ya gotta tell me, doc, is it possible for a man to be in love with an elephant?
Psychiatrist, using Viennese accent: No, it is not possible! A man cannot be in love with an elephant!
Soupy: (Whipping out a piece of jewelry the size of a hula-hoop)In that case, do you know where I can get rid of an engagement ring this big?
A pie comes out of nowhere, hitting Soupy in the face.

• • •

After several months on the air—it was just near the end of 1953 now—with the *Lunch with Soupy* show being so successful, the management at WXYZ came to me and asked me to do a show at night. At that time, Betty Clooney, Rosemary's sister, had been doing a nighttime show, which was all pretty much singing. She was leaving, and that's why they came to me. It was going to be a live show, on the air from 11 P.M. to 11:15 P.M., and the music was going to be provided by the Hank Treverson Trio.

We called the show *Soupy's On*, and it was a mixture of slapstick,

*In 1955, many of the world's best
Jazz musicians appeared on
Soupy's On:*

Top: *Me with trombonist Bill
Harris (left) and Dizzy
Gillespie.*
Above: *That hep cat, Henny
Sales, jazz clarinetist.*
Right: *Duke Ellington and me.*

sketch comedy, and music. We created a whole cast of zany, broadly satirical characters, in the irreverent tradition of Sid Caesar and Ernie Kovacs, to whom I've sometimes been compared.

Anyway, the characters I did on *Soupy's On* included Charles Vichysoisse—kind of a composite of Charles Boyer, Maurice Chevalier, and Charles Aznavour—a leering, oily "continental crooner" who was constantly arguing with his pianist and trading insults with surly patrons at the Club ChiChi. With a quick change I'd transform myself into Wyatt Burp, a seedy, power-belching sheriff, or the Lone Stranger, a fey, mincing cowboy hero. Then there was Calypso King Harry Bella, who was actually nothing at all like Belafonte, but a wild-eyed South American with a Moe Howard hairdo who made his living rolling drunks. We also had a spot called "Author Meets Critic," wherein I played host Ernest Hemingbone, a pipe-smoking writer who sniped at his literary rivals. I think, all in all, we must have created thirty or so different characters.

One of the great joys of the show was that I was able to invite many of the greatest jazz musicians and singers of the era, who often passed through Detroit as they toured the country in the mid-to-late 1950s. These were the halcyon days of jazz, when bop and bebop were sweeping the nation. Detroit had about twenty-two jazz clubs that you could go to every night of the week and catch somebody good. Among the greats who appeared and performed live on my show were Count Basie, Art Tatum, Dizzy Gillespie, Oscar Peterson, Duke Ellington, Ella Fitzgerald, Charlie Parker, Chet Baker, Lester Young, and Clifford Brown, who made his only televised appearance just before he was tragically killed, at the age of twenty-six, in a car accident while traveling to a gig from Philadelphia to Chicago in June,1956. (In fact, in Ken Burns' recent documentary *Jazz*, he used that clip from our show.) I can say without exception that they were all true professionals. And they had a fan in me: At the time, I had a collection of about three thousand records, consisting almost entirely of jazz and big band music. And I'm still a tremendous jazz fan and I attend as many performances as I can. But the guests on the show weren't limited to those from the musical world. Jerry Lewis, Milton Berle, and scores of other wonderful comedians also dropped by.

Of course, because the show was live, we had many memorable, unexpected moments. Once a week, we'd have to do the show from a different studio upstairs in the Maccabees Building, because they would be using our downstairs studio for a polka show and needed the space for the band. So, we'd be relocated to a smaller studio on the 14th floor. On this particular night, it came time to do a beer commercial. At the end of the commercial I was supposed to be pouring a beer, then lifting it and saying, "Altas Beer, to your health . . . " So, I'm just about ready to do that and the stage manager says, "Where's the beer opener?" And one of the stagehands, looking aghast, says, "I don't have an opener. I left it downstairs." Well, if we weren't able to do the commercial as it was written, we would have had to make good on it, which meant losing money by giving them a free commercial, so as you can imagine there was a little panic. Suddenly, a guy in a checkered jacket, with gray hair and a goatee, wearing an ascot and standing to the side, said, "Do you want me to open it for you?" So, I reach out to hand him the bottle and as he comes toward me I see that he's walking a little funny. He takes the bottle, puts his foot up on the table and I see that he has a wooden leg. On the inside of his wooden leg, he has a bottle opener. He opens the bottle, and that's the last thing that was said on that show. I fell down on the floor laughing. We never did find out who he was, but it was just about the wildest thing I ever saw.

It wasn't long until the station, seeing what a success we were, extended *Soupy's On* to half an hour, still live, of course. By this time it was 1956 and I was starting to make good money. For *Soupy's On*, I was making another two hundred dollars a week, so now I'm pulling in about four hundred dollars a week, and I'd also get another twenty five dollars for every commercial spot I did. The first year I was in Detroit I made about thirteen thousand dollars. The second year, I made about twenty-nine thousand dollars, and by the time I was ready to leave the city, I was making about two hundred thousand dollars a year, an enormous amount of money for that time, which made me the highest-paid local performer in the country.

. . .

RED WING RICK, a SOUPY FAN:

Soupy had the greatest show in DEEEE-TROIT. I remember eating lunch with him every day. Take your vitaminees. Cut the crust off of your bread, and drink your milk. Remember those Words of Wisdom. And who could forget White Fang, the meanest dog in Detroit, Black Tooth, the sweetest dog in Detroit; Willie the Worm, the sickest worm in Detroit; and of course, Pookie. Also, there was the guy who always showed up at Soupy's front door. "Telegram for Mr. Sales." The daily dose of pies. Peaches, Mildred, and Herbie the Elephant Trainer with Betsy and Bertha.

PETER STRAND, EXECUTIVE PRODUCER aND CO-WRITER OF "SOUPY'S ON":

I joined Channel 7, WXYZ, a month before we went on the air in 1948. Of course, in those days there were only a handful of television sets and I believe only nine cities, Detroit among them, had local TV stations. When Soupy debuted on WXYZ in 1953, we had been on the air five years, and whereas today probably over one hundred million households have TVs, in the mid-1950s it would have been remarkable if there were television sets in even six or seven million homes. In 1953, when Soupy arrived, I was an executive producer, but I was also doing some directing. Soupy was doing the noontime show, was a very gifted guy, and we recognized that very early and so we decided that we needed to use him more; actually, it was a matter of exploiting him a little more. That's how *Soupy's On* came to be.

We had Soupy and we had the Hal Gordon Quartert (which later became an octet)—Hal was the musical director of the station—and we had guests, but we knew that we needed more than that, so we decided that we'd do skits almost every night. Soupy and I wrote skits, but frankly, most of it was improvisation on his part, which was built around the outline of the scenario. We used actors from the *Lone Ranger*, which was on WXYZ-radio. John Todd, who played Tonto, would play the old-timer. Bertha Foreman would play the mother-in-law. Rube Weiss played Shorty Hogan. And Soupy was Charles Vichysoisse.

We also worked out a deal with Baker's Keyboard Lounge, a local jazz place. The deal was that we would promote the lounge and in turn, as part of their contract with stars, they would have them appear on *Soupy's On.*

Because we were a live TV show, there were many times when things didn't go exactly as planned. We were at the Maccabees Building and a few long-term sponsors, one of which was a local car dealer. We would have cars in the studios, different cars on different nights—with Soupy doing the commercials. I remember, he had a hand mike which would only go so far—actually, we thought it would go a little farther than it did—and one night he almost strangled himself with it. But he just continued doing the commercial. He went with the flow. We were laughing and crying at the same time, watching him. But nothing really fazed Soupy.

On the whole, I'd have to say that it was a very invigorating six years of doing live television. And at that point, you have to remember that essentially we had one of the only weekly live nighttime television variety shows for adults in the country.

SOUPY SEZ

Show me a jacket for an octopus and I'll show you a coat of arms.

What I really admired about Soupy was his ability to get close to his guests, his ability to really get down to their level of what they're comfortable with. He understood their language. He made these performers feel relaxed. And for him to do eleven shows a week, which included his kids' show every day and on Saturday, well that was a really exhausting record.

Certain guests stand out for me, but not necessarily due to their performances. We used to rehearse in the basement and the one day Billie Holiday was going to be a guest she brought her little Chihuahua with her to rehearsal. Well, the dog didn't bite Soupy but it bit me. I wasn't too upset by it but Billie Holiday sure was. The doctor came down and said that it might be a good idea to keep the dog in town to rule out the possibility of rabies and Billie wouldn't leave without him. So she canceled her appearances for two weeks and she wouldn't leave town without that dog.

Another time, I remember we were waiting for a rehearsal with the great Charlie Parker and he was late, very late. Actually, he didn't show up until the show was almost on. We asked what happened and according to his agent, Charlie was on his way to the studio and he

My people, let them eat cake! The man eating to my left is Clyde Adler, and next to him, the dapper gentleman with the moustache, is Pete Strand.

was enticed by a movie and he went in and started to watch it. He didn't stay long, just long enough to satisfy his curiosity.

During those years in Detroit, Soupy did a lot of guest appearances and I would go with him. It was amazing to see him work the crowds. They adored him. We would go to a Big Boy restaurant, one of our sponsors, and the crowd would be enormous. Soupy might just announce it casually on his show, "Hey, I'm going to be dropping by Big Boy on Ninth Avenue tomorrow afternoon," and thousands of people would show up to see him. And he'd stand there and sign autographs for a good hour. Other than a newsperson, it's rare for a personality to last on local television, especially for variety performers, but Soupy sure did. He was Mr. Detroit, for so many years. He could have continued on, but of course he had ambitions and naturally ABC was interested in him for network TV.

And remember, the Soupy Sales character we all know and love, was developed in Detroit.

. . .

After a while, things got a little tough for me because the networks saw that adults were actually watching TV at noontime, so they brought in performers like Peter Lynd Hayes and Liberace and put them on at noon and moved me to a morning time. It upset me because my audience was used to seeing me at noon and the whole concept of my show, which was lunch with Soupy, didn't really make it at eight o'clock in the morning.

But as it turned out it was the best thing that could happen to me because I didn't lose any popularity at all. The show was now called *Breakfast with Soupy*, and they also gave me an extra half hour—we were now an hour show—and we found ourselves up against some mighty good competition from the networks in the form of NBC's *Today Show*. But, using pretty much the same format I'd always used, we actually beat them in the ratings in Detroit.

We were so popular, that in addition to the two other shows I was doing—*Soupy's On* and *Breakfast with Soupy*—I was asked by management to add a third show on Wednesday nights, something they wanted to call *Soupy's Ranch*. They had no idea what they wanted the show to be, they just liked the name and figured I'd come up with some kind of concept. The show was just an amalgam of things I'd been doing all along, comedy bits like having someone ask, "Who's that stranger coming down the street?" and it would be me, riding a bicycle, wearing a cowboy hat.

CRISPIN CIOE, MUSICIAN—THE UPTOWN HORNS

Soupy Sales made an indelible impression on me because he was the only TV personality I cared enough to believe in. Other boomer kid-show icons—from Buffalo Bob to regional stars like Detroit's Johnny Ginger or the legions of franchised Bozos nationwide—still seemed like grown-ups playing down to us in funny clothes. Not so with Soupy. This was a guy with real improv/standup/adlib chops, a guy who could actually write comedy—and chose to do so for kids.

Here's a sequence I remember clearly from an early Detroit show: Soupy says, "Let's see what's on the radio this morning," and tunes in through static to an ad pitch that solemnly intones: "The Marines build men—drop us a line and we'll send you the parts." Suddenly Soupy's phone rings, he picks up the receiver, and a voice (the same voice as the one on the radio ad, but with a more urgent, nasal tone) barks out: "Hello, hello—is this the Fish Hospital? Well, let me speak to the Chief Sturgeon . . . " Suddenly there's a knock at Soupy's door, he opens it, "the arm" grabs him by the throat and its voice (the same one as on the phone but an octave lower and pushier) says: "Is your name Soupy Sales? Boy, have I got a deal for you today . . . "

All this quick-fire action took place in Soupy's "house," one of the show's most excellent features. No other adults or children ever appeared—probably because we, Soupy's "gang," were the real guests in his house every day.

Which is also probably why I, as a twelve-year-old in suburban Detroit upon learning that my family had moved into a house less than a mile from where Soupy actually lived, felt emboldened enough to ring his doorbell after a fierce blizzard and ask if he needed his walk shoveled. He said yes, paid me fairly, and this led to my

SOUPY'S WORDS OF WISDOM

Do unto others and then cut out.

*That's Tony on my lap at a Christmas party
at the Detroit station in 1955.*

*Michigan State Fair, 1955—Me passing out free bread at the
Silvercup Bread Space Ship. Wearing the millitary cap in the
foreground is Bill Caians, who gave away over 100,000 loaves.*

clearing his sidewalk a couple more times that winter, before he left the neighborhood for greener, less snowy pastures in L.A.. I remember feeling that shoveling that sidewalk only strengthened my spiritual rapport and ability to more fully savor the jokes on Soupy's show.

Decades later, as a musician touring with Robert Plant and the Honeydrippers in the mid-eighties, I met Soupy's son Tony at a party in the Hollywood Hills. I told him that he could never know how much his dad's show had meant to me as a kid, and he replied gravely: "Oh believe me, I know."

It's never easy or even all that profound analyzing comedy, but I believe that Soupy Sales belongs in the laugh pantheon that includes the Little Rascals, Laurel and Hardy, Abbot and Costello, Peter Sellers, and the Simpsons. Maybe he hasn't gotten that kind of recognition because his old shows weren't preserved or rerun or syndicated. Or maybe because low-budget kids' TV shows rarely get analyzed as art (the original *Pee-Wee's Playhouse* being a notable exception).

But I believe that millions of baby-boomers raised in the '50s and early '60s learned a lot about comedy and attitude from watching Soupy Sales on TV. Maybe his greatest gift was that he was the first entertainer who made us feel hip without wishing we were grownups. I can remember feeling that if I could start my morning with the *Soupy Sales Show*, I'd actually achieved something special that would stay with me.

I recently acquired some of the Rhino tapes of Soupy's old shows. The funny thing is, without any prodding, my seven-year-old daughter Katharine wants to watch them constantly. She finds Black Tooth monumentally hilarious, and said to me the other day, "Dad, were all kids' shows as funny as Soupy when you were a boy?" And all I could say to her was, "No, not even close."

· · ·

In 1955, I was catapulted briefly onto the national stage when the ABC network offered me the chance to be a winter replacement for Burr Tillstrom and Fran Allison's hit puppet show, *Kukla, Fran and Ollie*. Hastily, we put together a fifteen-minute live show and, still working from Detroit, we made the most of the opportunity—in several cities, as a matter of fact, we trounced the ratings *Kukla* had been getting.

In 1957, I was approached by ABC to do a national Saturday morning show, imaginatively called *Lunch With Soupy,* which would be sponsored by Jell-O. It was going to be the network's first non-cartoon Saturday morning show and the first network show ever to come out of Detroit. We were on at noon, and after we debuted, it was called by critics the fastest-paced show on TV and the hippest kids' show on television. I did most of the commercials and believe me, I sold a hell of a lot of Jell-O well before Bill Cosby tasted his first spoonful on TV. I remember once doing a commercial for Jell-O that lasted an incredible four minutes (okay, I got a little carried away, but somehow Jell-O just seemed to whet my comedic sensibilities), which they loved, of course. And why wouldn't they? It really didn't matter what I did or said about the product, the mere notion that they would get that much air time for their buck was good enough for them. In those days, you have to understand, things were pretty free and easy insofar as commercials were concerned. We knew what we had to say about the product, but there were no time constraints. Many of the commercials ran two, three, sometimes four minutes, and we'd just ad-lib like crazy, using whatever happened to be at hand.

The show was a big hit and suddenly I became much more than just a local TV star. Not only did I become even more popular in Detroit, but I also began to get exposure throughout the country. As a result, I started getting gigs I never would have dreamed of, like working the Little League World Series in Williamsport, Pennsylvania. I did some color commentating, while the ex–St. Louis Browns infielder, Buddy Blattner, did the play-by-play.

I thought that now that I was on the network I might get the powers that be to kick in a few more bucks for the budget, but that didn't turn out to be the case. The network never complained about anything I did, but we still had to do a show primarily with Scotch tape and baling wire.

In the meantime, I was, and I say this with all modesty, Detroit's biggest star—okay, I didn't have all that much competition, but still it was pretty impressive. I was treated royally everywhere I went—and there were some places I just couldn't go because it would be too much. For instance, there was no way I could just take my kids—Tony was now about seven years old and Hunt, who was named for my wife's mother's maiden name and was born on March 2, 1954, was four—to the movies—we would be mobbed. But I can't complain, because I loved it and I think I handled it pretty well. I tried not to let it go to my head. I did a lot of public appearances for nothing, just because I thought I owed it to the people of Detroit. And you know, even today, more than forty years later, there still exists a great love between me and the Motor City. I go back there at least a couple of times a year, and I'm still amazed at the wonderful reaction I get.

By this time, I was responsible for doing eleven hours of television each week. I was working so hard, I was meeting myself coming and going. I was doing a late night show and then doing the morning show, which was great, because I loved working, but unfortunately, there was a price to pay—and I wasn't necessarily the one who had to pay it.

TONY SALES, SOUPY'S OLDEST SON:

My dad was doing two shows a day, five days a week and resting the other two. So, we'd come home and have to be real quiet. Then, he'd be out late in the afternoon to do his night show. My brother and I didn't see much of him, becaues he was working all the time. So, we really didn't get much of a chance to interact with him very much, unless there were some new jokes to be told.

. . .

All this work and the attention it brought to me did take its toll on my family. Frankly, because of my grueling schedule, I was having problems at home, which were directly attributable to my work schedule. Let's face it. I was what today we call a workaholic. I just loved the business. It was like air to me and without it I could not breathe. I've sometimes thought about why this is, but I can't really come up with an answer. Is it because my older brothers never played with me as a kid and my mother worked all day, leaving me alone most of the time? Was my extroverted personality a way to gain the attention I didn't have as a child? I guess it would take a team of psychiatrists to figure that one out, because I just don't know. What I do know is that show business, as they say, was, is, and always will be my life. I was once asked what my hobbies were and all I could come up with was that I love westerns—I have a vast collection of Bob Steele westerns and I watch these over and over—and I love music, primarily jazz, and especially music from the big band era. I suppose some analyst might connect this and my performing to the need to be a child again, and if that's so, so be it, because in many ways I think in large part that's what's made me a successful entertainer all these years—the ability to tap into my "inner child," as they say, which in my case is pretty outer.

As far as guilt that I didn't spend as much time with my family as I might have, perhaps there is a little. But the truth is, I did spend time with my family—maybe not enough, although who knows what that is?—and I also had to provide for them, which meant spending time away from them.

Someone once asked me if I had any regrets, and if I could change anything, would I, and what would it be? Interesting questions. Of course, we all have regrets, but as for changing anything, the answer is, no. Because, if I did change one thing then everything else would change. I might not have had the career I had. I might not have met my wonderful wife, Trudy, or had my boys, Tony and Hunt. And so, I would not change anything because, bottom line, I am happy with the life I've led and continue to lead.

But enough philosophizing and now back to Detroit and my decision to make a change. I thought it was time I move on because I didn't want to be sixty, sixty-five and be sitting around one night having a drink and wonder if I could have made it in another market. And the timing was right, because I was separated from Barbara and that gave me the freedom to take a chance.

After a lot of thought, I approached the people from Jell-O and told them that I wanted to move to Los Angeles, and they said I could do the last fifteen shows out there.

And so, leaving my family back in Detroit, I packed up and moved myself and my cast of characters to Hollywood, a move that would eventually send my star soaring . . . at least for a while.

PART II

SPREADING MY WINGS

SOUPY SEZ

Show me an English policeman risking his life and I'll show you a Bobby Darin.

A hug from my buddy White Fang.

4

CALiFORNia, HeRe I Come!

LOS ANGELeS, 1961-1962, KABC

What? You found a fly in the raisin bread? Well, you just bring back the fly and I'll give you another raisin.

• • •

I went out to Los Angeles to do the final shows on the contract for the ABC-TV Saturday morning show for Jell-O, leaving my family back in Detroit. As I mentioned, my wife and I were having problems, and we both thought it would be a good idea to give the marriage a breather and see if we could somehow salvage the relationship. But I didn't go out to the coast alone: I brought Clyde Adler, aka White Fang; Bill Carruthers, our director; and a few other members of the crew with me. Ringing in my ears were the cautioning words of advice given to me by a well-meaning friend: "Don't let it excite you, but L.A. is a wild place. If you let it, it'll chew you up and spit you out." Well, I didn't really think that was much of a problem. After all, at heart, I was still that innocent kid from Huntington, West Virginia.

Burt Lancaster getting whacked with a pie, Los Angeles, 1962.

Once we got established, we did pretty much the same show as we did in Detroit, although there were a few differences that were a result of circumstances rather than choice. For one thing, our crew was bigger, which meant that there were more people to laugh at our antics, but it also meant that the show became a little less of a seat-of-the-pants operation. Another reason we couldn't be quite as loose with the show was that there were stronger unions out there. Certain things—camera shots, out-of-studio bits, and the like—had to be planned a little bit more in advance. Nevertheless, I think creatively the show was at the top of its game.

After the national show ended, I went to work at KABC, the local Los Angeles ABC station, doing exactly the same show—once again called *The Soupy Sales Show*, from 5:30 P.M. to 6:00 P.M.. Within a year, I'd built it into the number one program in what was one of the most highly competitive local markets. The show, which was especially popular with college kids, was slotted at night and the response was phenomenal—I was getting more fan mail than all the ABC network shows *combined*.

In 1962, the show was doing so well in the ratings that the executives from the station came to me one day and said, "Soupy, we want *The Soupy Sales Show* to go national on Friday nights, opposite *Rawhide*," which was a very popular one-hour western costarring a lanky young fellow named Clint Eastwood, a name that might be somewhat familiar to you. Being a lifelong cowboy fan, I had no problem at all facing up to a shootout against those fellas. In fact, I was looking forward to it.

With the new status as a national show in prime time came a little bit bigger budget, which allowed us to open things up a little more, which meant writing slightly more elaborate sketches and having more guests on, which meant that there was a bump up in our pie budget.

But none of this dizzying success could compare with the incredible luck that came my way one night as I was walking down Sunset Boulevard—which in itself was pretty incredible since no one in L.A. walks anywhere—and I was approached by a beautiful young woman about twenty years old. As she got closer, I recognized her as Nancy Sinatra, and the young man with her was her fiancé, singing idol Tommy Sands.

Tony Curtis gets pied. Los Angeles 1962.

Her face lit up when she saw me and she said enthusiastically, "My father is your biggest fan. Whenever your show comes on, he stops whatever he's doing—whether he's shooting on a movie set, at a cocktail party, whatever—just to watch you."

I was practically in shock. "You're kidding," I stammered—I mean, what do you say when you learn that the Entertainer of the Century loves your work? And for the Chairman of the Board to give up the cocktail hour to watch me? Now that was really something. I didn't really know what to say, so I just mumbled, "Thanks," or something just as creative, and went on my way. I was pretty surprised, because at the time I had no idea that people like Frank Sinatra were watching my show.

Nancy must have gone home and told her father that she'd run into me, because a few days after my chance meeting with her, I got a call. "Soupy, it's Frank"—and he didn't mean Nastasi, who was in New York at the time, pursuing his acting career—"I love you, I love your show and I want to come on, but I'll do it only on one condition."

I thought he was going to say that he'd come on so long as he didn't have to sing, or if I took the day off, or maybe if I gave him my first-born son. But that wasn't it. He continued: "I gotta get hit with a pie. And, oh yeah, is it okay if I sing?"

Okay? He hadda be kidding!

It was Frank's idea to keep it a secret. "Let's not tell anybody," he said, so his appearance was a complete surprise. Today, something like that would have been promo'ed for weeks, but back then we just didn't even think about things like that. The fact that Frank Sinatra, one of the biggest stars in the world, offered to come on my little show, was surprising enough.

I remember Frank showed up, without any fanfare, without any entourage. The director offered to show him around and Frank said, "Don't bother, I know the show better than you do."

The setup was going to be that he was going to come through my door singing his rendition of "A Foggy Day" (which he did brilliantly, I might add). Then, I was going to tell him what a great fan I was and all that kind of stuff. Then, there was a knock at the door. I go answer it and I get hit with a pie. I'm standing there and Frank says, "Who did that?"

"Dean Martin," I say.

Frank says, "I don't believe that." He goes to the door and gets hit with a pie, too. He wipes a bit of the pie off his face, tastes it, and says, "It's rum. It's Dean, all right." Boom, the skit's over. The whole thing took maybe five, ten minutes, and there was no audience other than the crew. The fact is, I didn't really like to work in front of an audience because it throws off your comic timing. The show was live—we couldn't go back and edit anything—so timing was of utmost importance.

Probably the most unfortunate thing about it is that there is absolutely no record of that first appearance. Like so many other shows that I've done over the years, the tape simply does not exist anymore.

The next day, it broke in the newspapers that Frank had been on the show. Suddenly, we were even hotter than we had been. There were photographs all over the newspapers and in magazines. *Life* magazine even did a whole spread on us. It was wild.

Frank was beautiful and his appearance gave the show an unbelievable lift. His guest shot marked the first time any show had beaten the ratings of my primary competition, *Rawhide*. Suddenly, it was hip to be on *The Soupy Sales Show* and get smacked in the face with a pie, and half the stars in Hollywood were lining up to get pied. Burt Lancaster, a sweet, gracious gentleman, wanted to surprise his kids with his appearance. For that reason, we taped the show we did with him, so he could be home, watching TV with his kids and seeing the surprise on their faces when they saw him walk out. Tony Curtis, who also wanted to surprise his kids, asked if he could play the flute on the show. Mickey Rooney appeared, as well as Jerry Lewis, Troy Donahue, and many, many others. And with all those star guests, everything went pretty smoothly. No complaints. Not the slightest sign of ego. Oh, well, I guess there was one exception to that. Robert Cummings came on the show and got hit with a pie. Fine. But then, a few days later, he actually sent me a dry-cleaning bill. He got paid a hundred and fifty bucks to do the show, and here he sends me a bill for seventy-five cents. Love that Bob!

After twelve weeks, though, our show was canceled, despite the fact that we were doing so well. Instead, they replaced us with a show called *Margie*, with Cynthia Pepper (not to be confused with *My Little Margie*, with Gail Storm). To this day, I can't give you a good reason why they did it . . . and if you have one, let me know.

THE ART OF PIE THROWING

There is a definite art to pie-throwing. You can use whipped cream, egg whites or shaving cream, but shaving cream is much better because it doesn't spoil. And no tin plates. The secret is you just can't push it and shove it in somebody's face. It has to be done with a pie that has a lot of crust so that it breaks up into a thousand pieces when it hits you.

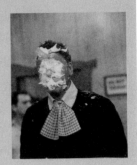

• • •

A lot of people ask me if the show or I changed because of the appearance of these stars, and the answer is no, at least not that I was aware of. In fact, I remained pretty calm. I must say, though, that it was a wonderful experience, because we were able to meet a lot of terrific people, people I never would have met otherwise.

Over the years, about twenty thousand pies have been thrown at me or people on my show. In fact, not long ago during an interview with Bob Costas on his NBC-TV show, he asked me about the effects of getting hit by so many pies, and I said, "I used to look like Cary Grant before all those pies." When all is said and done—and I hope that's not for a long, long time—I'll probably be remembered for getting hit in the face with a pie.

• • •

One of the most memorable moments on the L.A. show never actually made it to the air—although I didn't realize it at the time—but it now ranks as one of the classic outtakes in TV history.

I was supposed to be out front working with the dogs—White Fang and Black Tooth—doing different dance routines. There was going to be the sound of a woman's scream, and I would go to the door, open it, look down, and all we'd see would be a pair of women's shoes being pulled by cat gut followed by a pair of men's shoes. I

```
                CAST OF THE SOUPY SALES SHOW

                    Los Angeles (1961-1964)
White Fang                          Clyde Adler
Black Tooth                         Clyde Adler
Marilyn Mon Wolf              Clyde Adler
Herman the Flea                     Clyde Adler
Pookie the Lion                     Clyde Adler
Hippy the Hippo                     Clyde Adler


                     New York (1964-1967)
White Fang                          Frank Nastasi
Black Tooth                         Frank Nastasi
Marilyn Mon Wolf              Frank Nastasi
Herman the Flea                     Frank Nastasi
Pookie the Lion                     Frank Nastasi
Hippy the Hippo                     Frank Nastasi
```

would do a double-take to the camera and then there would be what we called a blackout and we'd go straight to commercial.

And so there I was, working out front with the dogs and there's the scream and I said to myself, "It's going to be fine." I start to go to the door and I see the number two camera swing around to my right and I thought, "Oh, good, he's going to get a close-up." Then I go to the door and I look down but instead of the shoes, which aren't there, I look up and I see a young woman standing there, stark naked, wearing only a hat, holding a balloon, and suddenly the sound guys start piping in "The Stripper," by David Rose. Then Clyde Adler grabbed the balloon and she started shaking her top. I saw that nude figure on the monitor and I thought, "That's it. There goes my career, my life, my family, everything." I wanna tell you, I just about had a heart attack, because I thought the whole thing was going on the air. As it turned out, they were merely feeding the shot of the girl into a videotape machine; the viewing audience never saw her, only the shocked reaction on my face. That tape, which is played in frat houses and bars all over the country, is one of the classic out-takes in television history and if you see it you can not only see the shock on my face, as I back away from that door as if I were shot out of a cannon, but you can hear the crew laughing (the Arts & Entertainment Network used this on their biography of me). And when I came back out front, there was no one there with me. They were all out in the back taking pictures of the girl. It's a good thing we weren't in color, because you certainly would have seen me blushing.

You know, today people ask me if she was completely naked and you know what, I really don't know, because I never went past the top of her. I was mortified, absolutely in shock. But today, of course, if something like that happened on TV, you'd probably say, "Honey, come on in and say hello to everybody."

I don't recall the young woman's name, although I think she was an actress who worked for Desilu Studio at the time, but she was dating our stage manager, Jimmy Baker. Imagine *that* telephone conversation.

"Hey, honey, we're gonna play a little joke on ol' Soup. Come on down to the studio and get naked."

"Suuuuure."

A few years ago, I was talking to Jimmy Baker on the phone and he told me the young woman's name and I looked her up and found that she's now married to some wealthy banker out in California. But I never bothered to get in touch with her. After all, what could I possibly have said? "Nice to see you again?"

• • •

Mr. Sales, Mr. Sales, you've gotta help me. It's real bad this time.
    My wife thinks she's a fish.
Well, why don't you take her to a psychiatrist?
You know you can't take a fish outta water.

• • •

After our twelve-week run, and in spite of terrific ratings, after the winter of the 1962 season, the show ended, and I went back to just doing my 5:30 kids' show. I thought we should have continued on the air, but I wasn't bitter about not being renewed. The fact is, I was just happy to be working.

Now, with my national exposure, helped by appearances on the show of people like Frank, Burt, and Tony, I was much more of a commercial commodity and, in an attempt to break out of being typecast as simply a kids' performer, I started to appear as a guest on sitcoms. I was on *The Real McCoys*, where I "played" the saxophone. That was a funny show! I played one of two jazz musicians whose car breaks down and we hang out at the house. George Lindsay was in it, too. I appeared in a couple of episodes of Nick Adams's Civil War half hour dramatic series, *The Rebel*, and I also appeared in an episode of *Ensign O'Toole*, playing a guy who was jinxed—every time I walked by something terrible would happen. In 1960, I did my first movie, called *The Two Little Bears*, at 20th Century Fox. It costarred Eddie Albert and Jane Wyatt. Randall Hood, who married Miyoshi Umeki (who co-starred in the sitcom *The Courtship of Eddie's Father* with Bill Bixby), directed that. I also appeared in a couple of movies, and did some guest appearances on various variety shows.

One day, someone handed me a sitcom script to read for a show they wanted me to consider starring in. It was, without doubt, the worst piece of crap I'd ever read. I said, "If I never work again, I still wouldn't do this show." Turned out, the script was for a little show called *Gilligan's Island*. Someone once asked me what part they wanted me for, and I answered, "Ginger, what do you think?" Of course, it was for Gilligan, the part played by Bob Denver. But I never, not for a moment, ever regretted turning that part down. It was an awful script and for the rest of my life, no matter what I did, I would have been identified as Gilligan, just as Bob Denver is to this day.

Two other projects I turned down were *The Incredible Mr. Limpett* and *Gentle Ben*. No, I was not going to be cast as the bear. They wanted me to play an assistant and, the truth is, at the time I thought I was much bigger than the character I was supposed to be assisting . . . and I was bigger than the bear, too.

I did one TV pilot that I did like and that I thought would have made a pretty good show. It was called *The Hoofers*, and I co-starred with Donald O'Connor. It was about two dancers who were trying to make it back to the big time. It was a great pilot and it should have sold, but it didn't. It was a big disappointment to me, but if it

Wink Martindale and I square off. One of us has been working out.

had sold I probably would never have made it to New York, and so I believe that in the end everything really works out for the best.

I was also brought to New York to host *The Tonight Show* for a week—in the period while they were waiting to bring Johnny Carson over to be the new permanent host—and I had the second-highest ratings, beaten only by Jerry Lewis when he hosted the show. I had a terrific time doing that—as I recall, the great insult comedian Jack E. Leonard was a guest, as were the Smothers Brothers and Gene Shepard—who I knew from our days together in Cincinnati radio—and who, on the show, played his head like a musical instrument, which I loved.

So, even though I didn't have a national stage anymore, I was doing pretty well, especially financially. On my local kids' show, I'd get a piece of every commercial we did, for products like One-A-Day Vitamins, Cocoa Marsh, and Bactine. This was actually quite unusual. Back in Detroit, I'd made a deal where I would get twenty-five dollars for each commercial that ran, but here in Los Angeles, I cut an even better deal, wherein I was getting 50 percent of the money that was paid for each commercial that ran. Not a bad piece of change.

• • •

I was mugging an old lady in Central Park,
When I dropped my cigarette in the dark.
So bruised and hurt, she lifted her head,
And "Those smokes of yours are the worst," she said.
Try a Punjab, and I'll be willing to bet.
You'll want to mug every other cigarette.
They're not too dark. Not too light.
Punjab's got a taste that's right.

That's right. That's right. That's right.

Well, I took her advice and her feeble hand.
And when she recovers, there'll be a wedding band.
Sure we'll mug folks together up in Central Park,
And I'll never forget her word to heart.
They're not too dark. They're not too light.

Punjab's got the taste that's right.

That's right. That's right. That's right. That's right. That's right.

—Phony Radio Advertisement

• • •

During my time in L.A., we made a record album called The *Soupy Sales Show*, which featured White Fang, Black Tooth, Pookie, and yours truly, of course. I was lucky enough to have it nominated for a Grammy in 1960. Unfortunately, I lost out to Leonard Bernstein's *Peter and the Wolf*, which pissed me off because that must have been done at least fifty times over the years, as opposed to my album, which was completely original. But my nomination did lead to something groundbreaking.

I was a member of NARAS, the National Association of Recording Artists, and every month or so we used to meet at a restaurant like the legendary Brown Derby. One day, I was sitting around with fellow members Sam Cook, Van Alexander, Les Brown, and Paul Weston. We were shooting the breeze, and I said, "Hey, guys, maybe it'd be a good idea to televise the Grammys."

"You're nuts," one of them said. "Who'd watch?" said another. "The networks won't touch it," said a third.

"Come on, it'd make a great show," I kept saying. But they remained unconvinced. That didn't stop me. A short time later I approached Jimmy Riddell, who was a vice president at ABC, with the suggestion. "I don't know if people are ready, Soupy," he said. A while later, I took the idea to Elton Rule, who was head of sales at the network and he had a slightly different reaction: "Sounds interesting," he said.

The next year, the Grammys were, indeed, televised. Coincidence? I don't think so.

All in all, I made six record albums:

The Soupy Sales Show (Reprise), 1961
Up in the Air (Reprise), 1962
Spy with a Pie (ABC-Paramount), 1964
Do the Mouse (ABC-Paramount), 1965

Bag of Soup (Motown), 1969
Still Soupy after All These Years (MCA), 1982

It's not easy to find the original albums, but recently I was fortunate enough to have several of them released on one CD by Rhino
records, and believe me, it's good to have them back in circulation.
A typical exchange went something like this (from *Up in the Air*):

```
Soupy: I'd like you to meet White Fang, the
       biggest and meanest dog in the United
       States.
White Fang: Araah-raah-raa-raa.
Soupy: What's that, you want a little bigger
       introduction?
White Fang: Araaah-araah-araah.
Soupy: Because you were the star of our first
       album? Okay. Here's a dog whose sounds
       will go to your head and to your heart—
       and they aren't going to do your stomach
       any good either.
Pookie: Hey, boobie.
Soupy: Oh, it's Pookie the lion. Here's Pookie,
       who lives by his wits. Liebowitz and
       Markowitz
Soupy: And here's Hippy.

       Silence.

Pookie: He's the greatest ad-libber since Milton
        Berle.
Soupy: I think this album has one comedian too
       many.
Pookie: Where should I forward your mail?
```

CO-PRODUCER OF "STILL SOUPY AFTER ALL THESE YEARS" AND SIDEKICK ON SOUPY'S WNBC-AM RADIO SHOW 1984-86:

From the end of the 1970s through the early 1980s, I was working at Casablanca Records and at the same time, the comedian Rodney Dangerfield, started to make it big again. I believed comedy albums could do very well if they were marketed right, and I wanted to sign Rodney to make a record and eventually Neil Bogart, who ran Casablanca, did sign him. However, I left the company before the album came out and I wound up back at MCA, where I had been previously.

So, during this period of time I was very anxious to do a comedy album, but I wanted to do something different, not just to sign up new comics; I wanted something unique, but I just didn't know what that was going to be.

One day I was driving to work and Soupy was on Dave Herman's morning radio show on WNEW-FM, New York City's most popular rock station, promoting an appearance he was doing at the Savoy, here in New York. Like most kids of my generation, I was a big fan of Soupy's. My friends and I never missed his show, and I had a great affection for this guy from my youth. And suddenly as if the lightbulb went on, I said to myself, "Soupy! He'd make a great album."

Immediately, I contacted the president of MCA, who was out in California, and asked him, "Do you want to sign Soupy Sales and do an album with him?" It turned out he'd seen Soupy at The Comedy Store in L.A. and had a fun night and so he said, "Sure."

So that's how the whole thing started. I called Dave Herman, whom I knew, and then he hooked me up with Soupy. I called Soupy and said, "I'm vice president of MCA, and I'd like to talk to you about maybe doing a record for us."

So, Dave Herman and I—Dave being the guy we both knew—had lunch with Soupy at the Friars Club. It was an incredible lunch. Soupy had us practically keeling over with laughter, telling us all these funny stories, telling these corny jokes, all of which were wonderful. What I was trying to do was find the album. So I always had a secretary with me, or my assistant or somebody, and, of course, they'd laugh and Soupy loves an audience. So, for example, when I got this Little Richard story out of him, and we're both hilarious laughing, then he started to embellish it. Over the next few weeks, we met with Soupy almost a dozen times for lunch to hammer out the concept for the album and, as I recall, he always ate and drank the same thing: filet of sole and white wine. Here was the idea we came up with: The album would be called *Still Soupy After All These Years* and it would be modeled after the Rodney Dangerfield album that was recorded live at his club, and after a live Joan Rivers album that Neil Bogart at Casablanca had recently put out.

This series of lunches was wonderful, and I said to myself, "Hey, you know if this project comes off, and we make this album, this will be great. But if it doesn't, this still amazing—to be able to say, twenty-five, thirty years later, that I had these lunches with Soupy Sales." It was like *My Dinner with Andre*, but instead it was, *My Lunch with Soupy*. I just wish we'd recorded those lunches.

So we talked about it, and what we decided to do was to make it a recorded version of his TV show, which had always worked on a dual level for both the kids and the adults. So, our idea was that we thought maybe we could make a dual album, both for the fans who are now middle-aged people and also as a kind of head-trip album for the fans of people like Cheech and Chong, or whoever might listen to this in an altered state. So, the question was, how would do we do that?

Finally Leon Tsilis, my coproducer on the albums, and I, said to each other, "Well what if we recreated the old TV show, audio-wise, but the references would be about today, and we'd have Pookie and White Fang and the Soupy's Words of Wisdom, but everything would be slightly slanted toward today." We thought this was the greatest thing in the world. So, I presented it to Soupy at one of these lunches and at first he said, "No, no—that's not—we're not doing. No, because you know, that was then and now is now . . . "

I thought, "Well, this isn't even worth trying to convince him." So, we said, "OK, all right, it was just a thought."

But finally, after a lot of discussion, we agreed that we'd do a combination of things from the old TV show and from his nightclub act, and that's what we did, recording it at the Bitter End, a legendary folk club on Bleecker Street in Greenwich Village, where comedians like Woody Allen and Joan Rivers had appeared early in their careers.

We got the best mobile unit around, the one Mel Torme used,

They wanted me to hit Lassie with a pie . . .
I decided to shake hands instead. L.A., 1960

Soupy: Now, what do we *mean* by that?
Crew: Yeah, what do we mean by that?
Soupy: You don't want to know . . .
Crew: Yeah, what do you mean by that?
Crew: Yeah.
Soupy: Frankly, my dear, I don't give a darn. No, what I mean is, people ought to read more books. Now, that may not seem like a novel idea, but please turn up the volume and let me state my case. I guess you could call it, a bookcase. Do you read me? Do you still have your set on?

I love literature. That's why I live in a ten-story building. And each one of those stories has a low ceiling. So they're all short stories. I read everything, especially poetry and rhymes . . . but if you don't like poetry, nothing could be verse. Because to me, there's no place like poem. In author words, a book can really change your life. Especially a checkbook. Okay, let's see what's new on the bookshelf. Right gang? Okay, here's a good book on gardening, with some good chapters in it, like:

- *How to Recognize a Dogwood Tree by Its Bark*
- *How to Have Dinner with a Cactus without Getting Stuck with the Check*
- *How to Handle a Creeping Charley without Slapping His Face*
- *How to Smuggle Fertilizer Across a State Line Before the Wind Changes*
- *How to Force Potted Plants to Attend AA Meetings*
- *How to Get to Know Your Fern, without Fern's Husband Finding Out*

because I knew that would make sense for two reasons. First, they'd do a great job, and second, I knew Soupy, who was such an incredible music fan, would love that we were using Torme's people. Anyway, we go down there, we pack the place with all invited guests and we recorded two shows, just in case. But when we listened to what we got we realized we needed more; it just wasn't enough material.

We were trying to figure out what to do when we remembered that there was that syndicated remake of a Soupy Sales show in California, and we realized that he had all that material that was written for that show. And although it was new material in the sense that it was more contemporary, it was still in the style of the old show from the sixties that everybody just loved. And so we went to Soupy and said, "You know, the album needs a little more, so how about if we go into a small studio with a small audience, and we record a couple of the bits of the guy knocking on the door. And maybe you could tell a couple of these great stories you've been telling us at lunch,"—which, in a way, was what we'd wanted to do in the first place—and Soupy agreed.

So one night we went up to a little studio in White Plains to save a little money and we invited about twenty-five people, and we recorded a bunch of the stuff from that show, including the guy knocking on the door—"Are you Mr. Sales?" "Yeah, what can I do for you?" kind of stuff, and White Fang and Black Tooth. And Soupy told some of those wonderful stories, too. The crowd absolutely loved him. And so, we had our album.

As it turned out, we had one other stroke of luck. At the time, MCA had acquired ABC records, where Soupy originally recorded his stuff. So, we were able to get the original song, "The Mouse," which was his hit song, as well as that wonderful song, "Pachalafaka." When I listen to that album now, I think it still holds up and I'm proud of what we did.

* * *

For a couple of years, back there in the early 1960s, what with my afternoon show and various guest appearances, life was pretty good in Los Angeles. I had made a solid bunch of friends, people like Hy Averback and Louie Quinn, and we used to hang out a place called Dominic's, which was a family-run restaurant where a lot of the writers and producers hung out. I'd also hang out with Dean Martin sometimes, because our sons played baseball

SOUPY SEZ

Show me a novel that is caught in a tornado and I'll show you a book that is Gone With the Wind.

together. I remember in 1963, opening day of the Little League season, one of the officials came over and asked Dean if he would like to sing the national anthem, and Dean said, "I don't even know the words to 'All of Me.'"

Sometimes I had to pinch myself to believe that I was actually hanging out with such a bunch of talented people like that. It was, I have to say, a very exciting time for me.

DAVE USHER:

Soupy's and my birthday aren't far apart—his is January 8 and mine is December 29, so we often celebrated together. During his time in California, while he was living in Beverly Hills, his wife, Barbara, arranged a surprise party and my wife and I flew out from Detroit. Soupy wasn't supposed to know anyone was around, so Barbara put us all in a bus and parked it in the alley between his house and the house of the bandleader Freddie Martin—for whom Merv Griffin used to sing. Everyone got on that bus and there we were waiting while somehow Barbara got him to come back toward the swimming pool. I think Soupy was quite surprised to see us all and I couldn't believe some of the celebrities who were there, including the wonderful actor, Lee J. Cobb. But I also notice that there were plenty of other people who weren't necessarily in the business. That's just the way Soupy was, he didn't care what you did for a living or how famous you were. If you were a friend, you were a friend.

. . .

White Fang: Raah-oh-raah-oh-raah.
Soupy: What's that you say, White Fang? Paramount keeps calling you about shorts?
White Fang: Raah.
Soupy: Did you leave your shorts at the Paramount Theater again?
A pie comes out of nowhere and hits Soupy in the face.

. . .

Like all good things, there must be an end, and in 1963 disaster struck—and I'm not talking about a California earthquake or a mudslide. Instead, there was a dispute with the station management. It's a bit more complicated than this, but essentially what it boiled down to was that the "suits," and by that I mean the salesmen, because that's who started running the stations, were moving away from live programming and toward videotaped shows. In other words, it was a lot cheaper to buy syndicated programs, let's say something like *The Rosemary Clooney Show*, rather than produce a show like mine, which, by the way, only cost about ten thousand dollars a week to put on, a pittance when you think about the budgets of TV shows today.

Another thing that might have affected my cancellation was the perception that I was undisciplined. But nothing could have been farther from the truth. Sure, when you tuned in it sometimes looked as if we were in the midst of chaos. But that was the point—it only *looked* that way. The truth is, in order to make it look as if the show was chaotic, that I was completely unpredictable, we had to be *very* disciplined. In order to create an environment where we could ad-lib and be loose, we had to be, in fact, extremely disciplined. It wasn't until I did *What's My Line* that people started respecting me, saying, "Well, he is intelligent." What they didn't know was that you couldn't be a dummy and do what I did all those years.

Another part of my problem was that I didn't really have anybody working for me. Looking back, it wasn't simply a matter of my making a mistake by not having anybody handling my career. It would have been nice, but who was going to handle me? In those days, there just weren't the kind of managerial services there are today. Sure, I had a manager who helped me put together a show, but in those days they weren't as sophisticated as they are today about shaping and guiding careers.

You might wonder why I didn't simply capitulate and videotape our show for syndication, but I just couldn't do that—it would have ruined the edginess and spontaneity that was largely responsible for the great ratings we'd always gotten. I know it sounds as if I wanted to remain in the Dark Ages, especially since so many shows were being videotaped and syndicated, but it's not that. I knew that my comedy was based in large part on its immediacy and I was afraid that I would get stale if I didn't maintain that immediacy. And so, the upshot was, our show was canceled. Now, nobody likes to get fired—it's a terrible feeling, as anyone who's ever gone through it can attest—but sometimes there are benefits. I believe it's good for everybody to get fired once in a while, because it takes you out of that realm of security where you feel like you're content and you don't want to do any more than you're already doing. The result is that you suddenly start to get a little sloppy.

And so, for the next year or so I had to rely on personal appearances and the money I'd managed to save over the years. Remember, I had a family—by that time Barbara and I had reconciled, and she and the two kids, Tony was almost eleven and Hunt was seven, had moved to Los Angeles to be with me—and a pool boy and a maid and a gardener to support. So, essentially, everybody was working but me. I did make some money doing those personal appearances, and I did an occasional guest spot on sitcoms or dramatic series like, *Burke's Law*, starring Gene Barry, but frankly, it was a very low, bleak period for me, perhaps the ebb of my career. I went through everything I'd saved for two years. Basically, I could not get a job. I could not get any work. I knew I had to make a move, but I certainly didn't want to go back to Detroit, because that would have been a step backward.

And it's at times like these, when you're down, that you get hit by a dose of reality, a sobering lesson about the fickleness of Hollywood fame. Most of my so-called friends, the same people who would come to my house, swim in my pool, eat my food, drink my booze when I was on top, wouldn't even bother to return my calls. It's really tough, because you can't believe that people you really, truly admire would treat you like that. But that only made me more determined than ever to get back on top.

And that's just what I did when one day I received a phone call that would have me move across the continent and into a new phase of my career.

Acting my brains out
Top: The Real McCoys
Right: The Rebel *(with Nick Adams)*
Above: McKeever and the Colonel

Philo Kvetch, New York, 1965.

5

New York, New York
The City So Nice They Had to Name It Twice

New York—1964-67, WNEW

An old man goes to a doctor and says, "Doc, I'm in terrible trouble."
The doctor says, "What's wrong?"
"I can't pee."
"How old are you?" the doctor asks.
"102," the old man answers.
"You've peed enough," says the doctor.

• • •

One day, in the summer of 1964, as I was sitting in my house wondering what the heck I was going to do next, I got a call from my manager, Stan Greeson, who asked if I wanted to go to New York and do my show. "I think I can get you a job with WNEW, Channel 5 in New York, for fifteen hundred a week," he said. I'd been making much more than that in L.A., but all in all that wasn't too bad a salary. Besides, I needed the work and couldn't wait to get out of California, because I'd had it with Hollywood. Out there, it doesn't make a damn bit of difference what you're going to do, it's what you've done and what you're doing right now. New York, on the other hand, was the place to be and the very idea of going there excited me and got the old juices flowing again.

Now let me take a moment here to get a little philosophical, a kind of Soupy Sez lesson about life. These were bad times for me, but I never lost hope. You must never let anything deter you. I've always, and I mean always, thought positively. And over the years the most important lesson I've learned is that if you can remain cool and never lose your enthusiasm, the world is yours. And that's just what got me through the bad times in Hollywood and led me to New York City, where, as it turned out, I was to have my finest hour . . . and also my most troubling relationship with the "suits."

The first thing I did when I got off the phone with Stan was to talk to my wife, Barbara, who was all for the move. The second thing I did was call my old friend and colleague, Frank Nastasi, who was now living and working in New York, to ask his opinion as to whether or not I should make the move.

"Frank," I said, when I got him on the phone, "I've got an offer to work in New York. What do you think?"

He didn't hesitate. "Soupy," he said, "they'll love you here."

As I was talking to Frank, something suddenly occurred to me. When I moved from Detroit to Los Angeles, Clyde Adler moved with me, but now he and his wife didn't want to move again. Clyde was primarily an engineer, and he never did have that much enthusiasm about working as a performer. He wanted to be an engineer. Certain people are performers and certain people aren't. Frank, however, is an actor who's made a living at it all these years. In fact, he's still acting today. And more importantly, I already knew him and his work. Frank was very, very good and what was even more important, we worked well together, which has always been crucial to me in any show business enterprise. I've never given a damn if someone was famous or how many credits they had or what big shot they were sleeping with or whose brother- or sister-in-law they were. The main thing is that you mesh creatively and personally. Frank and I did, and he was indispensable, not only as the voice of the hand puppets but as a human character in our sketches. He brought the same sense of absurdity to the show as he did to the great Shakespearean clowns. So, I asked him if he'd come back and work on the show with me. At first, he hesitated.

FRANK NASTASI:

After I left the show in Detroit in the late 1950s, to come to New York to appear in *Mr. Roberts*, I found that I loved it so much I decided to stay here. And then one day, I got a call from Soupy in California. He asked me how I thought he'd do in New York, and I said, "Oh, they'll love you here." Then, he asked me if I'd work with him on the show again. At first, I hesitated. I told him that I'd been doing legit acting and all that stuff, and I didn't think I could get back into the kind of groove necessary to do his show.

Soupy said, "Ah, c'mon, Frank you know it comes back. I'll tell you what, think it over a couple of days and then give me a call."

So, I thought it over and I said to myself, "Well, let's see, even at scale, that'll be good money—even for those days—and I know the show will be a success." So, I asked myself, "Why am I refusing?" I couldn't come up with a good reason, so I called Soupy back and said, "Okay, I'll do it."

. . .

Basically, I was being hired by WNEW to do the same kind of kids' show that I'd always done. It was going to be called *The Soupy Sales Show* and it started out as a half hour show, five o'clock in the afternoon, five days a week, with another hour show on Saturdays, when we were on from six to seven o'clock in the evening.

SOUPY'S WORDS OF WISDOM

Always buy thermometers in the winter time. They're much lower then.

We rented out our Beverly Hills house (didn't want to burn all my bridges) and the five of us—Barbara; Tony, 13; Hunt, 10; and Beauty, our standard poodle, and I—found a cramped apartment on East 68th Street, near the WNEW studio, and settled in for what I believed was going to be a real blast.

• • •

*Dine at the new quaint Italian restaurant, La Dolce Bellman.
And order their house special, Spaghetti Tarzan, which is actually brought to your table by a waitress in an ape suit. Order
wine by the bottle, by the glass, or if you're on a budget, by the
grape. La Dolce Bellman accepts either credit cards or playing
cards, depending on how dumb your waiter is. That's La Dolce
Bellman. Void where prohibited by law.*

—Phony Radio Advertisement

• • •

GENE KLAVAN, HALF OF THE POPULAR RADIO COMEDY TEAM OF KLAVAN AND FINCH, WNEW-AM RADIO:

I was working at WNEW on our show, *Klavan and Finch*, and when
Soupy first came to town, we'd promote him a little bit on our radio
show. One day, Soupy came up to the station and he was just fooling
around in the studio with us. He was one of those guys who was a
walking joke book. He had a gag for every occasion. He was hilarious.
And what's more, he knew how to use the medium of radio. His timing was very good, as opposed to someone like Jerry Lewis, who was
used to appearing live on stage and in the movies. Because I knew
more about radio than he did, I actually had to lead Jerry along and
he was never really good on the radio, although I have to tell you he
was wonderful about it. Soupy, on the other hand, was terrific, but I
guess that came from his early days of having his own radio show.

The first thing that got me, though, about Soupy was that my own
kids were watching him. In fact, I actually saw that infamous show
where he asked the kids to go into their parents' room and send him
the green pieces of paper. I thought it was hilarious. Of course, the station didn't think so and they suspended him for what, about two weeks?

At the time, Bennett Corn, who originally came over from radio—he
was from the sales department—was the station manager. He was a very
shy little guy, a terribly frightened guy. At the time, Metromedia was a bad

bunch, completely salesman dominated. In fact, Finch and I were fired several times from our show. I remember, they brought a guy in named Harvey Glascock—an apt name—and he did the same thing to us.

[Let me interrupt here just to say that the comedian Buddy Hackett had the best line I ever heard when he heard the name Harvey Glascock—"I hope he doesn't fall down . . . "]

They tried to proscribe and prescribe what you would do and what music you would play. It was creatively very stifling and we fought it all the time. At times, we virtually got into fist fights about it. Anyway, one time they fired us and we went over to talk to John Kluge, the big boss, at his apartment. Well, we talked to him for a while, and he sold us on accepting the fact that we were fired, and then we sold him on the fact that we weren't fired. In any case, we went back on the air and they replaced the station manager. The people over at the TV station were just as bad. They were a tough bunch, all absolutely terrified all the time—afraid of not making their quota. Afraid of losing their jobs. And as I've always said, God protect me from a desperate man.

Meanwhile, when Soupy got suspended, Finch and I thought it was great. We had a ball with it.

One day, when Soupy was already rolling along, he invited a few of us, WNEW disk jockeys, up to his show. Finch and I rarely made appearances, but it was really the thing to do at the time. Soupy had everybody in town on that show, so finally he got to us. It was Willie B. [William B. Williams, a disc jockey on WNEW-AM], Finch, and myself.

I can remember the sketch because I've still got photos. We were in our French restaurant, Chez Bippy. Willie B. was the maitre d' and Finch was sitting at a table. I came in wearing a top hat and tails, nothing fancy, kind of crappy looking, in fact. Willie B. welcomed me and then, somehow, he had me cause a ruckus in the place, at which point he hit me with a pie. Finch got up to defend me, but he didn't hit Finch with a pie, he hit Willie.

One thing about Soupy and being on his show: His tempo was incredible. It was constantly moving and he was constantly moving and he had constantly these characters coming through the window, which also added to the pacing, which was breathtaking.

. . .

With Frank Sinatra and director Al Caaell at the talk-through before the show.

Me, Frank, Sammy Davis Jr., Trini Lopez.

More pie, anyone? That's Frank Nastasi in the middle.

Are you looking for a job with a little bite to it? Then enroll today at Vito's Famous Dog Catcher School, where their motto is—"We jump from our cars and put your dog behind bars." At Vito's, you learn how to get the cocker out of a locker, how to make a beagle legal, how to train a collie to say, "Golly." Show a poodle how to use its noodle. And teach a Spitz not to. Enroll today at Vito's famous dogcatcher school. If pain persists, see your doctor.

—Phony Radio Advertisement

• • •

I don't want you to get the wrong idea. In some respects, working at WNEW was fascinating and extremely stimulating. The station boasted some terrific talent, people who knew how to do something more than just show cartoons. There was Sonny Fox, who went on to become a successful producer; Sandy Becker, known for such zany characters as Hambone and Norton Nork, who passed away a few years ago; and a burly young guy, still only in his twenties, named Chuck McCann. A gifted actor (brilliant in a tragic movie role costarring with Alan Arkin in *The Heart Is a Lonely Hunter*), Chuck was also a fine mimic who specialized in both Stan Laurel and Oliver Hardy and had a great deal to do with promoting a revival of interest in their films. Throughout my time at Channel 5, the support staff—engineers, directors, and the crew—were fabulous, the best in the business.

But almost immediately, I began to run into problems with management, and it didn't take long for me to realize that I was now working for the worst station in the world. To put it mildly, management at the time was horrible. They had their own style of what they wanted and here I came along and I just wanted to do my show, which had been the top-rated show in Detroit and Los Angeles, and they resented that. I believe they put me on in the afternoon just to spite me . . . they couldn't care less.

The trouble started as soon as I went on the air. First, they called me in and said that they thought for at least the first month I shouldn't throw any pies. Can you imagine? In large part, that was how I made my reputation and now they were asking me to suppress one of my trademark bits. I couldn't believe it. Then, they called me in and told me that the dogs—White Fang and Black Tooth—were growling too much. "What's that supposed to mean?" I said. "Nothing is too much if it works." And it *was* working. But what the hell did they know?

I found out later, all this brilliant advice was coming from the salesmen, whose primary contribution was that they were getting drunk on their six-martini lunches and then imparting their wisdom to the station managers. It used to be that the business was run by creative people, but then they were phased out and the salesmen took over the stations. The owners would say, '"Well, this guy can bring in five or six million, let's make him president of the station." So they make him president and he doesn't know a tap dancer from a trombone player—they just don't have that gut reaction to say, "Let's go with this, I think it'll be great." Instead, they started taking polls and surveys at the preview houses. You know who goes to preview houses, don't you? It's the same people who used to go watch *What's My Line?* When we were at the old Ed Sullivan Theatre—which now houses *The Late Show*, with David Letterman—we'd get eight hookers, six winos, and Miss Miller, who was an institution in those days, an inveterate talk show junkie, who would appear in the audience in shows like Merv Griffin and *The Tonight Show*, when it was in New York. These people would go anywhere, sometimes just to get out of the cold. And these were the people who would go in and rate the shows—you know, push the button on the right if you think it's funny. You can't have eighteen or twenty people be the criteria for whether or not a show is gonna be a hit. Put it on the air and let the people decide. I remember when they gave Howard Cosell, of all people, a variety show and it went into the toilet. Their conclusion was, hey, people didn't want a comedy-variety show. Ridiculous! Of course they do—they just didn't want to watch Howard Cosell!

You know, the great Duke Ellington once said it best a long time ago, and it goes for everything, whether you're reading an article in a magazine or watching a show, and that is, "It don't mean a thing if it ain't got that swing."

The advice about dog grunts and pies wasn't the end of the madness. Next, after that first month's moratorium on pie-throwing was over, the "suits" called me in and said I was throwing too *many* pies. I was practically in shock. I'd say, rhetorically, "How are we in the ratings?" I knew the answer: We were number one, and there wasn't nothin' wrong with that.

But then, to top it off, one day I noticed that the crew wasn't laughing during the show, which was kind of disturbing to me. I started to doubt myself a little. Was I still funny? Finally, I went up to one of them and asked, "What's wrong? Isn't this stuff funny?"

"Sure it's funny," he said, "but we were told not to laugh."

"Who told you not to laugh?" I asked.

"The station manager," he replied.

"What the hell's he doing that for?" I blurted out. "This is a comedy show, isn't it?"

The truth is, since we never did the show with a live audience, the crew was my audience, and I used them to judge whether the bits I was doing were funny. By not laughing, they were killing my timing. Incredible!

The bottom line was, from the moment I got there, the "suits" were constantly fighting me. This was something I had never experienced in my entire career. Everywhere else I'd worked, I'd pretty much been left alone. And everywhere I'd ever been, leaving me alone paid off in tremendous ratings and popularity. This was the first time I had come upon management that was difficult, and it made my life miserable.

Somehow, though, despite all the interference from the station's executives, I managed to muddle through. The show became popular almost immediately, and creatively, I think I was probably at my peak. I think the secret of our success in New York was a marvelous creative synergy. It was obvious as you watched the show and saw the wise-cracking interplay between me, Frank, Eli the prop man, Art Siedel the producer, Lennie our floor manager, and Artie Forrest, who directed many of the shows (and more recently worked with Rosie O'Donnell). Fortunately, management had to back down on their edict for the crew not to laugh, and now the loud hoots of laughter on the set were genuine—the show was live and you just can't fake that kind of chemistry. We were having a blast and it showed.

I was doing six shows a week, writing them all in advance, in longhand on a legal pad. Then we'd spend a day going over each show with the producers, especially to make sure that we'd have all the necessary sound effects and props (inevitably including empty pie shells and cans of aerosol shaving cream). There were no rehearsals, just a talk-through or production meeting, as we called it, in my office, which, by the way, was not exactly the executive suite. My dominant decorative motif was to press my name all over the walls with a rubber stamp; there was one piece of rare, fine art: a poster depicting a line of naked men, captioned, "Will the real Soupy Sales turn around?"

We generally started the production meeting about 2:00 P.M., after Donna Duckwall, my lovely and brilliant secretary, had hauled in the usual mountain of fan letters, each one of which was answered, if not by me, then by a member of the staff. During the meeting, we'd go over the script I'd written, and it was a freewheeling brainstorming session. If someone—Frank, Artie, Eli, even Donna—came up with a better line or a sharper bit than what I'd come up with, we'd use it. There was no ego involved. The point was to put the best show on the air that we possibly could. By 3 P.M., we'd go into the studio for our one and only camera run-through. Then it was show time.

I was asked about the peculiar appeal of the program in "Love in the Afternoon"—not the Gary Cooper-Audrey Hepburn movie, but a very flattering profile of me and the show that appeared in the *Sunday New York Herald Tribune* magazine. The piece was cowritten by David Newman and Robert Benton, who a couple of years later hit the Hollywood jackpot when they collaborated on the screenplay for *Bonnie and Clyde*, starring Warren Beatty and Fay Dunaway. Benton, of course, went on to direct *Kramer vs. Kramer*, with Dustin Hoffman, and *Places in the Heart*, with Sally Field. (I like to think that I gave them their start.) In the article, I made the point that because of changes in American society and popular culture, children could no longer be entertained by cartoon jockeys. You had to be creative. Even then, at a time that seems innocent now—just before the explosion of anti-Vietnam protests, drug use, and free love—kids were growing up faster than ever because of what they were seeing on network television. Love scenes, lingerie ads, a general slackening of the old censorship codes. You couldn't play down to kids anymore.

. . .

We did the sketch and sure enough, as I remember, there were like seventy-five pies thrown and it took hours to clean the studio, it was totally destroyed. And it was one of funniest moments I'd ever seen.

—Art Seidel

. . .

One night, I was out at some night spot and Frank Sinatra walked up to me and said, "Hey, Soupy, don't you like me anymore?"

"What do you mean, Frank?"

"Well, I was wondering why you haven't asked me to come on the show."

"Frank, the first time's a favor," I said, "the second time's an imposition."

"I'll be the judge of that," he said. "Write a pie sketch for me, and I'll come on the show."

So he came on in 1965, and this time he brought Sammy Davis and Trini Lopez with him. It was a classic bit and, I'm happy to say, you can see it today because there is a tape of that appearance.

It was absolutely wild. Frank, Trini, and Sammy were guests at *Chez Bippy*, a fancy French restaurant. I played the waiter and Frank Nastasi played a bratty little kid who was there with his father, the celebrated disc jockey William B. Williams (of WNEW-AM radio's *Make Believe Ballroom* fame).

At one point, Frank and Sammy and Trini come in and sit down and I, playing the waiter, come over to them and Frank says, "That's the rudest hatcheck girl I ever did meet in my whole life. We came in here with our hats and coats and I even gave her a Picasso and she didn't even give me a claim check."

"What hatcheck girl?" I say. Frank gets up and says, "I'm gonna call the police." Then I say, "I'll take care of it." Then I go over to the phone, dial and say, "Hey honey, we have a sorehead here—bring it back!"

Soon, there were pies flying all over the place. Trini Lopez, smacking me with a pie after Frank gets hit, says, "You can't do that to my band leader!" *Bam!*, I take one in the face. And then Frank, playing the kid, says, "I'll show you who's your leader," and then, *bam!* He hits Trini with a pie. And then someone hit Sammy with a pie. And then it was mayhem. Everyone on the set was covered with aerosol pie. And the funny thing is, we told Sammy not to wear his own jacket, but he insisted, and I think, after it was all over, he was a little sorry about that. It was a free for all. I think we used two hundred pies on that show. There was shaving cream everywhere.

. . .

Sung to the tune of: "Catch a Falling Star":
Catch a pickled herring, put it in a barrel, save it for a rainy day . . . Catch a pickled herring, put it in a barrel, watch the neighbors move away!

. . .

FRANK NASTASI:

I had never met Sinatra before, but he and I shared the same dressing room. When he met me for the first time, he actually called me "Frankie." But I didn't call him that, because I knew he didn't like being called "Frankie." Just Frank.

The bit took place in the restaurant we had, Chez Bippy. See, *Laugh-In* stole a lot of our stuff, because George Schlatter used to watch our show. He used the word "bippy," and the waterbed bit with Judy Carne, when she gets hit, Soupy used that all the time. And, there was another thing they stole—the talking pictures. And you know what, after our show went off, and their show was still running, they never once asked Soupy or me to be on the show. That hurt.

Anyway, we didn't have a particular plan as far as the pie throwing was concerned. I was playing a kid and I was standing on a chair—and I was having a very good time, everybody was throwing pies at everybody else. And then a guy comes by with a pie—I'm not even sure I knew who it was—and I pick up one of the pies near me and *pow!* I hit Sinatra! He was a little stunned, because I don't think he expected it from me. And those pies—you know what they're made of—they were made of shaving cream. Before they were egg whites. And they were messy. But see,

125

with the shaving cream, you put water on it, and it evaporates. So I hit him and then it just became a wild free-for-all—I think we used up two hundred pies in all. Shaving cream was all over the studio.

• • •

Within four months of arriving in New York, I recorded my third record album, *Spy with a Pie*, and Frank Nastasi "appeared" on the disc with me. This was the height of the sixties espionage craze, with James Bond, *Our Man Flint*, *The Man From U.N.C.L.E.*, *Get Smart*, and others. I wrote the book for the album as well as wrote a couple of songs, but Lenny Whitcup and Ted Lehrman wrote the music. We had all the top musicians in Hollywood on that because the guy who was Frank Sinatra's accompanist helped hire the musicians.

As the record rose up the charts, I began to be booked for special appearances. One Saturday afternoon, someone from the Paramount-ABC record company called and said they wanted me to go out to Stern's department store in Queens and make a public appearance to sell some albums. And it was at this point that for the first time, I realized just how popular I'd become.

An hour or so before I was scheduled to appear, a car picked me up and we drove out there from the city. No one went with me, not even my own management—it was just me and the limo driver. As soon as I arrived I saw hundreds of kids milling around outside, waiting to get in. It was nuts. There was a line, of sorts, but scores of people were breaking through the line.

As soon as I could find the store manager, I asked, "What about security?"

"Oh, don't worry, Mr. Sales," he said. "We've got plenty of security." They had so much security, in fact, that the crowd went nuts, broke through all the barricades and started ripping off the records. It was probably the most stolen album of all time. And there I was, right in the middle of it, trying desperately to sell some records and sign some autographs. It got so bad that the security guards, what few of them there were, all left in fear of their lives and suddenly here I am, entirely on my own, caught up in a mob scene straight out of *Potemkin*, with an army of kids desperately trying to get to me.

Finally, someone said to me, "We can't hold them anymore, run!"

Roosevelt Field, 1965. No officer, I've never seen this woman before in my life.

The Macy's Thanksgiving Day Parade, 1964, one of three that I was in. Why they had me on the rocking horse is anybody's guess.

So, that's just what I did. I literally ran for my life, out of the store, headed toward where I thought the car would be to take me back to New York City. There, standing outside the door, was the driver, blissfully playing with himself, while the limo was parked out in the lot.

"What the hell are you doing?" I screamed at him.

So now, all I can do is make a break for it, toward the car. But as I was bolting through the parking lot, pursued by the crowd, I tripped and fell, finding myself on the pavement with hundreds of screaming kids surrounding me. As I was lying there on the ground, one of them started beating me over the head with a paper cylinder. I looked up at him and asked him—quite reasonably, I think—"Why are you doing that?"

"I just want to touch you," the kid replied.

Boom! That's when I knew. That's when I knew just how popular I was, popular enough that my fans just wanted to get close enough to touch me. It was wild. After all, I was always in the studio. It was as if I were hermetically sealed. I went from my house to the studio and then back to my house—so I had never experienced anything like this.

I was also given one of the ultimate New York honors when Macy's invited me to ride along in their Thanksgiving Day parade in 1965. Somehow, they managed to misplace my float, and I wound up riding on the hood of a black limousine (thankfully, not driven by the same guy who took me to Queens). Still, the Macy's people told me I was the hit of the parade, and I've got to tell you it was wild playing to a crowd of about a million people. At one point, a little kid ran up to me looking totally confused and said, "Hey, Soupy! How'd you get off TV?"

I think the natural question to be asked, after episodes like these, would be to find out if I let this popularity go to my head. The answer is no. Letting success go to your head is a luxury very few people can afford. Once you do that, I think you stop being creative; you stop growing as an artist. Instead, you start being concerned only with your reputation, as opposed to the value of the work you do. Now, I'm not saying that I didn't like or appreciate the popularity, because I did. But I tried not to let it affect me in any way. I just went back and did my job to the best of my ability. The truth is, creatively I was quite happy. Sure, I would have liked to have a bigger budget and less interference, but I think I was at the top of my game, insofar as performing and writing were concerned. I was also very much appreciative of the way the audiences responded to me. They were great, absolutely great. We were obviously doing something right, because by 1966 our show was syndicated in fifty television markets in Canada, Australia, and New Zealand.

. . .

People thought of him as one of themselves. He was a star, yes, but he was an approachable star. He had that homey quality that people identified with and I think that was partly responsible for that whole cult thing.

—Bob Talbert, Columnist for Detroit Free Press

. . .

FRANK NASTASI:

Our show in New York was different from the show we did in Detroit, because we weren't a kids' show at all, even though kids watched us because they loved the pie bits and the falls and all that slapstick kind of stuff. They also loved the different characters and personalities who came on the show. But the adults loved us because of some of the performers who came on the show. We had every major singing group, like The Supremes, the Vandellas, Ronnie Spector and the Ronettes, Judy Collins, Jackie and Roy, and Jack Jones. We also had many of the top comedians, like Fat Jack Leonard, Nipsey Russell, and Henny Youngman. Soupy got along well with these comedians. Fat Jack Leonard wouldn't pay attention to anything; he just did what he wanted to do. But he was funny. I remember Henny Youngman was on the stage before the show playing his violin, and I said, "What are you doing?" And he said, "I'm rehearsing." And I said, "Henny, you've been doing that for a hundred years! And now you're rehearsing?"

We also had a lot of actors on, too. They weren't all used to the improvisation that we did on the show and so, if they wanted it, beforehand, we would sit down and say, "Ok, this is the bit, and this is how you're going to be included."

Of course, we had White Fang, Black Tooth, Pookie, Hippy, Peaches, and Nut-at-the-Door, which was really many characters. And I would do them all. I would say, "I did everything on the show except work Soupy's head."

There were new characters added too, for the New York show. For instance, there were Hobart and Reba, who lived in the potbelly stove. This is how it came around. We were fooling around one day, and Soupy was backstage, behind the set. During the commercial break he came out and had this head in his hand, and I said, "Where'd you get that?"

He said, "I found it backstage and there's another head back there, too."

And I think a stagehand brought out another head, so that we had a male and a female. And this was happening while the commercial was going on. Soupy said, "So, what do we do with them?" And I said, "Put it in the stove. And you'll open it up and say hi to it."

So we put the head in the pot-bellied stove and at one point Soupy goes over to the stove and opens it up and there's that head, which we called Hobart, and he says, "Hey, what are you doing there?" and I said, from off-stage, "I'm here because I couldn't find an apartment." And that got a big laugh from the crew, so we kept both heads in there and every once in a while when Soupy was probably thinking of something to do, he'd go over to the pot-bellied stove, open it and say "Hi!" and we'd start a bit with Hobart and Reba.

```
Hobart (played by Frank Nastasi): Hey you know,
       I'm pretty happy.
Soupy: Yeah, what are you happy about?
Hobart: Well, I'm happy because my son is this big
        baseball star.
Soupy: Your son?
Hobart: Yeah, he's with the Hot Stove League.
Soupy: How's he doing?
Hobart: Well, his coach is raking him over the
        coals.
Soupy: Yeah, yeah. So tell me, how long has he
       been a baseball player?
```

Hobart: Oh, about a year now. Oh yeah, he's a minor you know.

Soupy: Oh, is that right?

Hobart: Yeah, that's why he can't get in the big leagues. He's a minor.

Soupy: Is that why they're raking him over the coals?

Hobart: Yeah. Ha, ha, ha.

Soupy: I just threw that in.

Hobart: Yeah, well throw it right out . . . really. He learned a lot about baseball, but not from me.

Soupy: Well, who did he learn baseball from?

Hobart: Well, Reba.

Soupy: Your wife Reba?

Hobart: Yeah.

Soupy: Well, what about her inspired him to get into baseball?

Hobart: She had a lot to do with it, see, because she's got baseball eyes.

Soupy: She's got baseball eyes?

Hobart: Yeah, two of them . . . but you know what, I hope he makes good. Those baseball players, they make good money, they get very wealthy. Take Willie Mays for example, Mays is in oil. Mickey Mantle's in oil. Ted Williams is in oil.

Soupy: Well, what about your son?

Hobart: He's in hot water. Yeah, they caught him—for stealing a base.

Soupy: Well, there's nothing wrong with a baseball player stealing a base.

Soupy: Oh, there's Reba.

Reba (also played by Frank Nastasi): Wait a minute, both of you stay still.

Soupy: Well, are you going in or coming out?

Reba: Stop. Will the real dummy please stand up?

. . .

FRANK NASTASi:

We had some other new characters, too, but they weren't always on screen. There was Luigi the Ice Cream Man—He would say, "I gotta go now, I gotta go to the Ponderosa!" Soupy would say, "The Ponderosa Ranch?" Luigi would say, "No, I'm gonna ponderosa in the mouth if she don't have my supper ready!" The truth is, we didn't always know what we were gonna do, and that was one of the fun things, just because we didn't know. We'd say to ourselves, "How do I get outta this?" And somehow Soupy or I would come up with some line that would work. Many times we would break each other up, and not intentionally. I'd say, "Well, what were you laughing at before, I didn't do anything funny." And Soupy would say, "No, but the look on your face when you said the line was worth it."

We did do a lot of crazy things over the years. Once, as a kind of take-off on the Naked Woman episode in Los Angeles, I did the Naked Man. I knocked on the door, Soupy opened it and there I was dressed as Dracula with the big, black robe on. As soon as I saw him—and remember, I wasn't on camera—I whipped open the coat and I was naked. All Soupy said, was, "YOW!" and every time he said, "YOW!", I'd go, "1,2,3 . . . " and whip open the coat again.

In New York, I'd have to say that White Fang was the most popular character on the show. Even today, you mention Soupy and his show and, even more than the pies, people remember White Fang.

After a while at Channel 5, we were pretty disillusioned because we didn't get support from the studio. We were doing the show on a shoestring budget, and one thing that forces you to do is to become more creative. You have to think of other things you can do if you don't have the money to do the thing that you want to do. And sometimes that actually works to your advantage, creatively, I mean.

Soupy's popularity was contagious, and it didn't take me long to realize how popular we were, Soupy because he was Soupy and me because I was part of his show. I was once invited to play in a celebrity baseball game—it was sort of like a club fund-raiser. I was the only "celebrity," although I certainly didn't consider myself famous.

Ed Sullivan and me doing "The Mouse" on his show. It was the first time in eighteen years that any star was invited back a second consecutive week.

6

THANK GOODNESS NEW YEAR'S DAY ONLY COMES ONCE A YEAR

At the time, we thought it was just another one of Soupy's jokes.
—Art Seidel, Producer

It made him even bigger than if they hadn't suspended him.
They had thousands of kids picketing the station every day.
—Al Cassel, Director

• • •

I'll tell you one thing, my enormous popularity did come in handy in the aftermath of that fateful New Year's Day, 1965, when my career seemed tottering on the brink of extinction, a day that has now gone down in television history. Unfortunately, the episode itself was destroyed long ago. There have been varying versions of the story, but here's how I remember it.

Holidays never meant much to me, you know. I mean, I just liked to work, the more work the better. But on this particular New Year's

Day evening, I would have preferred to just stay home and watch football, but I was told that because of the holiday we were going to have a skeleton staff, which meant that, "You're not going to do the show with your usual set."

"You can't do a show without a set," I said.

"It's okay," they said, "you can do the show with a lavaliere mike instead of the boom mike."

"I can't do that. It ruins the whole illusion of the show if I'm walking around with a mike."

Well, I tried to argue them out of it, to cancel the show for that day and give everyone the day off, but they wouldn't hear of it. So, we went on.

It was few minutes before seven and we were just coming out of a commercial break and the director comes over to me and says, "Soupy, when we come out of commercial we're gonna have about a minute left. What do you want to do?" Well, I was writing all the shows, and if I could save a bit for the next day rather than burn for one minute of air time, I'd do it. So I said to the director, "Well, I'll just ad-lib something."

So, we came back from the break, and Lennie, the floor manager, pointed to me. So, I moved up as close to the camera as I could, and I said, "Hey, kids, last night was New Year's Eve and your mom and dad were out having a good time and it's only right, since they work hard all year long. And they're probably still in the bedroom asleep. Now, what I want you to do is tiptoe into the bedroom and don't wake them up and you'll probably see your mom's pocketbook on the floor along with your dad's pants. Now, be real careful, because we don't want to wake them up, but I want you to go into your mom's pocketbook and your dad's pants and you'll find some little green pieces of paper with pictures of guys with beards on them. Now, what I want you to do is take those little pieces of green paper and put them into an envelope, and on the envelope, I want you to write, Soupy Sales, Channel 5, New York, New York, and you know what I'm gonna send *you* in return? A postcard from Puerto Rico."

Well, I'd done a version of that bit before, back in Detroit, I think, although not on New Year's Day, of course, so I didn't think anything of it. I just went home that night, the way I always did.

But a couple of days later, all hell broke loose because some woman from New Jersey wrote a letter to the FCC and sent a carbon copy to the wonderful folks at Metromedia, who owned Channel 5. She claimed that I was encouraging the kids to steal. Now the truth is, kids are a lot smarter than we give them credit for. They knew I was fooling around. Sure, I got lots of dough, almost eighty thousand, as a matter of fact, but except for a few actual dollar bills—which, by the way, we put into the Jerry Lewis canister for muscular dystrophy—all of it was Monopoly money.

Oh yeah, and I did get a buck from some twenty-eight-year-old who said, "I've seen your show and you *ought* to go to Puerto Rico."

Well, after that letter the shit really hit the fan. Jack O'Brien, a TV columnist for the *Daily News,* and a terrible, terrible man, turned on me (after his hateful columns, I never spoke to him again). He called for my dismissal. Let me digress here for a moment, to say a few words about critics in general. A critic can be very powerful on matters dealing with the stage and maybe in movies, but critics have absolutely no power whatsoever in making or breaking a television show or performer, because the people who watch the show either like what they see or they don't. They can judge for themselves and nobody can tell them any different. That's why so many shows that are torn apart by critics can still become big hits despite what's written about them. So you see, I have no problem with criticism per se. It's lies and cruelty that I abhor. When I read an utter lie about myself in the paper, and there have been some of those, believe me, I'm very disturbed about it. Criticism is one thing, a lie is something else. First, I get steamed, but then, fortunately, after I put it in perspective, I'm able to calm down. But in this particular case, Jack O'Brien was just way out of line in calling for my dismissal. He was messing with my livelihood and that's just plain wrong. Now don't get me wrong, it's not that I had a problem with all critics and gossip columnists. The fact is, Walter Winchell was always very nice to me—and he wasn't so nice to everybody. But O'Brien's style was to put everybody down, and that doesn't set well with me.

Anyway, one day not long after the episode, I walked into the studio and I was told that the executives wanted to see me upstairs. I didn't know why, and I know this is going to sound incredible, but

I actually thought they were calling me up there to give me a raise. Far from it. Instead, there were maybe ten guys and suits up there waiting for me, along with Muriel Reese. They asked me, "Did you go on the air and ask the kids to send you money?"

"Yeah, I did." And, when I added that I'd received almost eighty thousand dollars they practically went into a catatonic shock.

One of the suits said, "You're suspended."

And then I was the one in shock. "I don't believe it," I said. But I knew they weren't joking. They sent me home and told me not to come in for two weeks and in my place they put on Fred Scot and Chuck McCann, filling the air-time with cartoons and things like that.

This, if you haven't gathered by now, has been a recurring theme in my career. I've often had trouble with management. It's not that I was working against the establishment, it's just that the establishment always branded me as undisciplined, which was pure bullshit, because as I've pointed out before, to do the kind of show I did, you had to be incredibly disciplined.

Well, as soon as people found out about it, they went nuts. I mean to tell you they jammed the switchboards; people came over by the hundreds, carrying placards that said things like "TYRANNY AT WNEW-TV." They threw eggs and tomatoes and paint and that was just my *family*. But seriously, folks, there really was a groundswell of support, a lot of it from college students. I also had a few other champions. On the *Les Crane* TV talk show, my friend Orson Bean leaped to his feet and said, "You know what the best kiddie show on television is today? Soupy Sales! That's right! And critics like Jack O'Brien knock him. Soupy Sales! The man is a great clown in the tradition of *commedia dell' arte!*" The studio audience went wild.

I was very depressed about the whole thing. No one likes to be

SOUPY'S DEFINITIONS

Apple turnover— a command a fruit peddler uses when training an apple.

Bacteria— the back door of a cafeteria.

Blue jeans—tight pants that tell dirty jokes.

suspended, especially for something that was so innocuous and, when you think about it, ridiculous. As I said, kids are a lot smarter than we give them credit for. They knew it was a joke. They knew I wasn't encouraging them to steal.

Anyway, after a few days I got a call from one of the executives. "You've gotta come back over here and speak to the people picketing outside. Ask them not to throw paint. They're going crazy."

There was no way I was going to do that. As far as I was concerned, they created the situation, let them deal with it. But something good did come out of all this, because I realized how much my fans cared about me, and let me tell you, that was almost worth all the aggravation I went through. It was enormously gratifying, and it's something that I'll never forget.

I was off the air about two weeks before they capitulated and asked me to come back. Remember, though, it wasn't out of the goodness of their hearts. They were just responding to the incredible pressure the fans were putting on them to get me back on the air.

Let me say this: Over the years it's become a big thing. I don't care where I go—even today, thirty-five years later—someone will say to me, "I sent ya ten dollars," or, "I sent ya twenty dollars." Who had money like that in those days? If I'd have gotten all the money that I was supposed to have gotten, I'd be on an island somewhere with a harem!

In the end, it was the best thing that could have happened to me, not only because anytime you get fired or suspended you find that people tend to take your side, but also because it shakes any complacency you might have developed. And the added bonus for me was seeing how much my fans cared for me. It was something I'll never forget.

Chestnuts—People who are crazy about Dolly Parton.

Dialogue—how you make a phone call to a tree.

Operating room—Warren Beatty's bedroom.

Stopwatch—the command a policeman gives to a Rolex who's going too fast.

Bewitches—the way people in Brooklyn say, "I'll be right there"—"I'll bewitches in a second!"

139

FRANK NASTASI:

I've heard Soupy talk about the New Year's Day incident, but I don't think he remembers exactly the way it really happened. Of course, sometimes, we're both bound to get our facts wrong, but in this case I know the story a little better than Soupy because he was just busy trying to think of something to get him through the end of the show. Here's the way I remember it.

We had asked the studio, the cheap studio, which, by the way, was owned by one of the richest men in the world, John Kluge, if we could have New Year's Day off—just put on some cartoons and stuff, because, we argued, everybody knows it's a holiday. They wouldn't do it, because tape was expensive then. So we said, "Okay, we'll just wing it."

Being a holiday, it was a skeleton crew that day, because those who did work got double time or whatever and the studio wanted to cut down on the number of people they had to pay. So we come into the studio and we were all kidding around with the cameraman and the crew, making it all just part of the show.

I was off-camera that day, but you could hear my voice. For instance, I would play a stagehand, which I often did because stagehands weren't allowed to say lines, because then they'd have to be paid, and our budget didn't allow for that.

Anyway, we came back from commercial with a minute or two left, and Soupy says, "Well, everybody here with your bloodshot eyes,"—meaning the crew—and things like that. And then he says, "I'll tell you what gang," we always called the audience "gang," not "boys and girls," because we knew we weren't just a kids' show; we knew that a lot of college kids and people in their twenties watched. In fact, we were probably more of an adult show, although the kids watched and liked some of the farcical stuff we did—"Go into your mom and pop's room and go into their pants and pocketbooks and get me the pieces of paper with George Washington's picture on it. Send it to me and I'll send you a picture postcard from Puerto Rico." That's all it was.

Anyway, all hell broke loose when some lady complained that we were preaching to kids on how to rob. We were suspended for ten days, Soupy without pay, and me, suspended with pay. But suddenly, and believe me, we never could have predicted this would happen, we were heroes. The people, mostly college kids, came and they picketed the studio, yelling things like, "Freedom of Speech" and all that. They were going wild. And we couldn't do anything about it.

I thought it was ridiculous that they took him off for something like that, but in those days, and maybe today, too, though to a lesser extent, I think, you had to do things for everyone who complained about something. Also, we were always being accused of saying lines that were not very nice. Like, "I climbed up a tree and kissed my girl between the limbs." That kind of stuff. We never said them. Those are myth—in those days, they'd throw us off the air so fast.

Frank's absolutely right about those myths. There were all these other things I was supposed to have said, like "What begins with 'F' and ends with 'UCK' . . . a firetruck," or, "I took my wife to the ball game and kissed her on the strikes and she kissed me on the balls," or, "My wife is a great cook, she makes great pies—I eat her cherry and she eats my banana." And people would swear that I said it! Now, you know that in those days you couldn't say nuthin'. Come on, I'm an intelligent man—a college graduate. You know, people act like dummies a lot on television, but there are no dummies on television—you couldn't be a dummy and do a show.

After many years, I think I finally figured out how these ridiculous stories got started. Kids would come home and they'd tell a dirty joke, you know, grade school humor, and the parents would say, "Where'd you hear that?" And they'd say, *The Soupy Sales Show*," because I happened to have the biggest show in town. And they'd call another person and say, "Gladys—did you hear the joke that Soupy Sales was telling on his show?" and the word of mouth goes on and on, until people start to believe that you actually said things like that.

I got so annoyed at these stories that I used to have a standing offer of ten thousand dollars cash to anyone who could prove that I said any of the things that people claim I've said.

SOUPY'S WORDS OF WISDOM

Never hit a man when he's down. Kick him, it's easier.

Look, at every TV station, whether you know it or not, there's a little spool in the master machine in engineering that records everything that's said, everything that goes on. And believe me, if I said half the things I'm supposed to have said, they would be on some blooper record making the rounds.

THE WEATHER REPORT

Soupy: All right gang, let's find out what the weather's going to be like today.
He switches on his radio.
Radio Announcer (played by Frank Nastasi): It is time once again for *As the World Burns*, the continuous story of human drama in the little town of Hunger, North Dakota. Tonight marks a very special milestone for us here on *As the World Burns*, for tonight is the fifteen thousandth show of the series. The longest continuous show on radio. And now, *As the World Burns.*
Soupy: I love this show . . .
Radio Announcer: Now, you may remember, Harry had split up over a dispute concerning Marie's third husband John who was the brother-in-law of Minnie, having married Minnie's sister Margie, right after the automobile crash which injured Tag's wife Ramona, who left her job at the bank to go on an archeological expedition . . .
Soupy: I remember that . . .
Radio Announcer: . . . with Dr. Forest, who in reality, is Virginia's brother, the man who Lillian left Archibald for three weeks after Mitch left Hilda for . . .

Soupy: Oh, he did that? I was sick and missed that . . .

Radio Announcer: . . . and their little daughter, Faith . . .

Soupy: Oh, Faith, what a beautiful girl she is, that Faith.

Radio Announcer: . . . and in the second show . . .

Soupy switches the channel.

Radio Announcer: Here we are with the new cigarette of the day. Each cigarette is ten feet long and it filters through chicken wire at each end. If you find you do not like them or cannot get used to them in this forty-eight hour test, throw them away, you'll never get your money back.

Music again plays: "Well, I'm walking . . . I'm feelin' so blue, I smoke cigarettes . . . I'm losing my sleep over you . . . "

Soupy switches the channel.

Radio Announcer: Welcome, to your home food service, the program that helps you set out a meal fit for a king. And if your husband feels as if he's really not a king after all, you can pound him with it. Remember the words of Carlton Fredericks, who said, "Make him a roast beef, or make him a steak. Make him a pudding or make him a cake. Make him a ham on a hickory roll. And if he complains, well then, make him a frog." So then, housewives, when you make an upside-down cake, does the flour rush to your head? When you cook vegetables, do they go too fast? When you make a chicken gumbo soup, do you ask him how he likes gumbo soup? These and many other questions will be answered for you, by your food expert, Gaspar Gaspain, yours truly.

Our first question today is from a Ms. Judy Mitchell, who asks, "Dear Mr. Gaspar Gaspain, entrepreneur, gourmet par excellence, and man who knows about food, sir. Is it permissible to use artificial citrus flavoring in my cooking?"

"Dear Ms. Mitchell, not only is it permissible—it is recommended for the prevention of artificial rickets."

Soupy switches the channel.

Radio Announcer: And here is today's weather.

Soupy: Here we go with that weather.

Radio Announcer: Present temperature is eighty-four degrees.

Soupy: Ooo, wowie, yowie-boo.

Radio Announcer: Then it's cooler tonight.

Soupy: Oooh . . .

Radio Announcer: Lowest temperature's in the sixties.

Soupy: Oh, yes.

Radio Announcer: Sunny and pleasant Wednesday, the high will be in the mid-seventies.

Soupy: That's it?

Radio Announcer: That's it. That's the weather for today.

When we started the new show after Soupy's suspension, I think Soupy came back with, if you can imagine, even more energy than he had before, because now he had something to prove.

—Art Seidel

. . .

When I returned after my suspension I felt rejuvenated, yet things weren't much better at the station because every time I turned around I was fighting with them. Often, it was about the budget. It was like pulling teeth from a chicken, and chickens don't have any teeth.

Nevertheless, they weren't stupid. They had just witnessed proof of how popular the show really was—hey, they still had paint all over the outside of the building, just in case they needed a visual reminder. So, they moved our time slot again. Now, we were pitted against the highest-rated news show in the country, the Huntley-Brinkley report. But, never fear, we still managed to hold our own, and the added competition just made me even more determined to do the best job I could.

· · ·

On April 16, 1965, only a couple of months after my suspension on Channel 5 was lifted, I was booked for ten days to do the *Soupy Sales Easter Show* at New York's Paramount Theater. Traditionally, the Easter week is supposed to be suicide, not only because of Easter but also because of Passover, which is usually around the same time.

On the bill with me was Little Richard and his relatively unknown guitar player named Jimi Hendrix; the Hollies, with Graham Nash; Shirley Ellis, singer of "The Name Game"; the Hullabaloo dancers; the Detergents; and the King Curtis Band. A surprise to most people, although it wasn't to me, was that we broke the attendance record that Frank Sinatra had set a generation earlier. The headlines read: SOUPY SALES AND THRONGS OF TEENAGE FANS REVIVE THE PARAMOUNT! People had been waiting around since something like two in the morning, just to get in. The size of the crowd was so overwhelming that *Time* magazine reported, "The crush broke the glass on the cashier's box." We made something like $295,000 in ten days. They were carrying the money out in bushel baskets and cardboard boxes. There were mounted police all over the place. We thought there was a riot.

My appearance at the Paramount was probably my greatest thrill in show business, because the Paramount Theater had been closed and they opened it up for the Easter holiday and the Jewish holiday, and everybody thought they were nuts for doing it. It was really wild.

Making time with "Edwina" Sullivan.

Me with Tab Hunter on the New York show, 1965.

Besides the show, they also had a movie, *The Wackiest Ship in the Navy*, with Jack Lemmon and Ricky Nelson. The show lasted more than three hours, and we were doing five shows a day, which was insane. So, the promoter of the show called us in after the first show and he said to us, "The show is running too long. What I want everybody to do is cut down your act to ten minutes, because we've got so many acts in the show." And then he turned to me and said, "Soupy, you can do fifteen, eighteen minutes, whatever you like."

SOUPY'S WORDS OF WISDOM

Be true to your teeth and they won't be false to you.

I said, "I'll take all the time you'll give me—eighteen minutes. That's fine. That'll be great." I didn't think anything else about it. Someone gives me eighteen minutes instead of ten, I'll take it every time. But, what I didn't know, was that Little Richard got very upset at this, because he thought that I'd gone in and said I didn't want him to do more than ten minutes. Well, I love Little Richard, I mean I used to play his records and I used to have Pookie do a lot of his hits on the show, and believe me, it really helped out.

The next day I arrived at the Paramount and I saw that there were police all over the area. Of course, with the crowds we were pulling in, we'd always had plenty of cops around, in the front, in the back, but now there were extra cops and they seemed to be patrolling the area. Now we were a sellout and all that, but still there had never been so many cops around. Anyway, I'd walk around and I'd say to them, "How you doing?" and they'd hardly acknowledge me and then they'd walk right off, real fast.

I was getting ready to go on and I asked the stage manager, "Hey, why are all the police here?" and he said, "Well, Little Richard is upset because of the time limitation, and this morning, before you got here, they had to eject him from the theater, and he was holding himself down in the elevator and he said he wasn't going to leave because he was going to do fifteen minutes, not ten. And the promoter said, "You're only doing ten." And Little Richard said, "I'll get even with Soupy." So they threw him out and they got rid of him on the show." I asked the stage manager, as I was getting ready to go on,

147

The future Mrs. Soupy Sales.

"Why all the cops? There are so many of them."

"Haven't they told you?" he said.

"No."

"Well," he said, "Little Richard is upset. He thinks you're the one who got him thrown off the show and they say there are a couple of guys out there looking to knock you off. Yeah, they're in the balcony somewhere. The cops are trying to find them. But you don't have to worry, Soupy, the cops are all over the place."

Somehow, this didn't particularly make me rest easy. In fact, it was kind of bothering me, this possibility that there were a couple of guys up in the balcony with guns who were trying to cut my career short—listen, I figured that was always the job of the "suits"—so I decided that the only thing I could do to protect myself was to move around *real* fast.

So, I get ready to go out there on the stage, and the first number I'm going to do is called "Your Brains Will Fall Out." The music starts: *doom-doom, doom, doom, doom-doom de loomy-doom* and then the announcer says, "Here he is, Soupy!" and the crowd is going crazy. I go out there onstage and I'm moving man, I ain't standin' still and don't think the rest of the performers don't know about what's taking place. King Curtis is leading the band, and as I go by him, he only half-whispers to me, "Get away from me, man. Don't stand next to me, man." But I figured as long as I kept moving, and as long as I stuck near him, over to the side, I'd be safe. So, I'd walk over to the side, where he was, and he'd try to get away from me, saying, "Stay away from me, turkey." But I stuck to him like glue and all the while he was going crazy. Finally, I said to him, "If I'm gonna get it, you're gonna get it.

"Don't dance in front of me," he said. He was going absolutely crazy.

Of course, in the end, nothing happened to me, but damned if the cops didn't catch a kid with a gun, lurking up in the balcony. I never pressed charges. Years later, it came out that Jimi Hendrix had told everyone that I was jealous of Little Richard and wanted him off the bill, which is bullshit. I was never jealous of anyone in my life. I've always encouraged good talent. Nice talent. Talent that doesn't hire a hit man.

FRANK NASTASI*:

During the course of the show, we appeared on *The Ed Sullivan Show* with the Beatles. At the time, we were the hottest show in New York, so it was natural, I think, that Sullivan would have us on. When we showed up, we were mobbed. It was pandemonium. So much so, that he had us back on the next week. And it was during that show that Soupy first met his present wife, Trudy.

. . .

In the 1960s we had all the great singers, Joan Baez, the Beatles, the Rolling Stones all doing important songs about society, peace and love, social unrest. And Soupy was singing "The Mouse." "Hey, do the Mouse, yeah, you can do it in your house, yeah.

—Comedian Perry Gardner, at Soupy's 75th Birthday Tribute at the New York Friars Club, Janurary 2001

. . .

During the show one day, I was fooling around with some music, coming up with different dances—since 1959, when Chubby Checker had the Twist, I was always coming up with all kinds of silly dance. I'd do "the Indian," the "Bunny Rabbit," "the Motorcycle," and for one of them I put my fingers up to my ears and started wiggling them and called it "The Mouse," which was a takeoff I'd dreamed up on "The Monkey" and other teen dance crazes of the time—you know, everyone put their hands up to make mouse ears and flashed their buck teeth.

"Hey, do the Mouse, yeah . . .

"Hey, you can do it in your house, yeah . . ."

The two guys who wrote the song for me had written all of Frankie Valli's big hits. Well, it caught on—I did a recording of the song—and it kind of went through the roof. In New York, they sold a quarter of a million copies in one week, and in Los Angeles, they sold twenty-five thousand copies in a single day. I even managed to win a Grammy Award.

I was booked on *The Ed Sullivan Show* several times, and once, on the bill with me were the Beatles, who were appearing on American television for the first time. We were on the same night as the comedy team of Allen and Rossi when Paul McCartney performed "Yesterday." Sometime later, when the Beatles were out in Queens, playing Shea Stadium, they drew fifty-two thousand people. That same afternoon, I was at the Singer Bowl and I packed the place. I had eighteen thousand people there. I often said that Flushing was tilted that day, from all the people.

To tell you the truth, I didn't particularly enjoy doing the *Sullivan Show*, because he was a big pain in the ass, and as a result, doing his show was a royal pain in the ass because he made us do our acts over and over again every day. What happened was that you would start out on Tuesday, and by Wednesday everyone on the stage was laughing themselves into tears. But by the weekend, it had all gone flat because everyone knew all the bits by heart. And that's just when Ed would stroll in demanding a lot of changes. Or, what sometimes happened is that because you'd do it over and over again by show time it just wasn't funny any more to him and he would cut the act out of the show.

Ed Sullivan was every bit the odd character he was reputed to be. I did the show four times, and each time he would say to me, "Have you met my wife, Sylvia?" By the fourth go-round I said, "Ed, I know her better than you do."

One time, I was invited on the show to do the Mouse. That night, the Sullivan people decided it would be cute to put a couple of plants in the audience, a couple of women who, when I went into the audience, would get up and do the dance with me when I came by. Well, one of them was a young woman named Trudy Carson, who I found out later was a dancer with the June Taylor dancers, who used to appear on *The Jackie Gleason Show*. The plan was that I'd do the Mouse and then the camera would swing over to them in the audience, and they'd be doing the Mouse, too. I was married at the time, so I think I just nodded to her backstage, or something like that. And that was it. I didn't see her again until two or three years later when I was doing *Hellzapoppin'*, and by total coincidence she was in the show with me as a dancer. I remembered her, of course, and as you can imagine, she remembered me—after all, how many times had she been in the Ed Sullivan audience doing the Mouse in front of millions of people? When I separated from Barbara in 1967, we started to go out.

It was pretty wild, because we pretty much got along perfectly right away. We had a lot in common. I enjoyed beautiful things— she was a beautiful thing. And she had a good sense of humor, which of course was necessary if she was going to go out with a guy who looked like me. She was also the most un-show-business person I'd ever met, which was important to me because I always used to hang around more with the behind-the-scenes people, like the writers, producers, and directors, not other performers.

TRUDY CARSON SALES:

I had been a Rockette and I was now doing the *Jackie Gleason Show* in Florida, as a member of the June Taylor dancers, with whom I'd been dancing for two years. It was my first week back in New York City after the television season had ended, and I received a call for a kind of strange job. They wanted me to be a "plant" in the audience at the *Ed Sullivan Show*. I was supposed to do a little thing with Soupy Sales and the truth is, although Soupy doesn't like to hear this, I didn't even know who he was. When I was down in Florida, I don't remember watching any show on TV but the *Gleason Show*.

Anyway, they told me something about Soupy Sales, that he had this television show that was a big sensation. I was going to get up in the audience and do the Mouse with him, and I had no idea what it was. They said, "All you've got to do is get up and wiggle your fingers when he comes by and looks down at you."

I remember getting ready in the dressing room on the second floor of the Ed Sullivan Theater and I heard screams coming from outside. I looked out the window and I saw a big limo with a lot of kids following it and screaming. The reaction was like something the Beatles were getting at the time.

I saw Soupy at dress rehearsal and I thought he was pretty cute.

Everything went great during the show, which, by the way, I never actually got a chance to see, even though I'm sure there's u tape of it floating around somewhere.

. . .

*Mr. Sales, Mr. Sales, you've got to help me. It's my wife. She
thinks she's a piano.*
Did you take her to a psychiatrist?
No. Do you know how much it costs to move a piano?

. . .

One of my favorite segments on our show was "Philo Kvetch," a
broad parody of the old detective serials with their cliffhanger end-
ings that I used to love when I was growing up. I thought it might be
fun to create a character like Philo Vance from the mysteries written
by S. S. Van Dine and played by William Powell in the 1930s film
series. I called him Philo Kvetch. It started out as a one-time thing
but it got to be so popular that I thought, "Well, we'll do fourteen
chapters, with a weekly cliffhanger," hinging on Philo's pursuit of a
master criminal called the Mask. And then that got to be so popular
that we wound up doing thirty-nine episodes. Each episode lasted
about ten to fifteen minutes during the show. It turned out that it
was the first time anyone had ever done a continuing serial on TV.

After a while, we even took the serial on location. We shot at
Yankee Stadium and at a shipyard, all kinds of different locations.
We had lots of guest stars, too: Totie Fields, Joan Rivers, Henny
Youngman, Chester Morris, Cliff Robertson, Alan King, and Huntz
Hall, one of the Dead End kids. For the finale, we wanted to get
Arthur Godfrey to play The Mask—who was, of course, unmasked
at the end. But Godfrey was too busy, so we got a gentleman who
made a brief, meteoric career for himself impersonating Nikita
Khruschev. It was a great segment. The series was so popular that we
had the idea of looking for somebody to put up money to make it
into a film, but unfortunately, that never happened.

For the most part it was an ad-lib kind of thing. I wrote the general outline of what was going to happen, major lines, things like
that, so that we had a general idea of what we were going to do, but
as usual, improvisation played a major part.

. . .

FRANK NASTASI*:

"Philo Kvetch" was a wonderful series of sketches. Soupy's idea was to do a skit that would focus on the old-fashioned gangster type, with fedora hats and trench coats, the whole bit. I was, among others, Onions Oregano. It's interesting how that name came about and it illustrates how we created a lot of stuff that went on the show. We'd come into the studio and right away we'd say, "What can we do with this bit here?" And someone would say, "Well, we've gotta give the detective a name." And Soupy came up with "Philo Kvetch." Burt King, the cameraman, was there with us, and we were trying to come up with a name for my character. Now, I had a habit of flipping an onion up into the air—don't ask me why. Remember when George Raft did that thing in the movie, Little Caesar, with flipping a coin into the air? Well, I used to toss an onion up in the air. I guess I was hooked on onions. So, Burt says, "Let's call you, 'Onions.'" So, I had my name, Onions. Then someone said, "Okay, but what's his last name? He's got to have a last name."

And Burt King says, "How about Oregano?"

And it was like the lights went on in the place. "Yeah," we all said. "We like that." So, that's the way Onions Oregano was created. And he was a real dumb character. I always remember the first episode, when Soupy was the Mask, the arch criminal, and when he'd get mad at me, he'd shoot me in the shoulder. Well, the first time it happened, it was an inspiration, he shoots me and I go, "Don't worry boss, it's only a flesh wound." And we'd be laughing so hard. We'd just stand there and laugh.

I appeared in almost every episode of the series. Once, I had to double as the Mask and Onions Oregano. I remember, when we went to Palisades Park, we had to go on the roller coaster, but Soupy didn't want to go on it, so I took his place, wearing the mask and the outfit. First I played the Mask, and then I played Onions Oregano.

Most of those episodes were ad-libbed. Looking back, some of them were beauties. Some of them were pretty corny. We always said, "We'll do anything within the realm of possibility." And that's just what we did.

• • •

With my arms around two beautiful women, one of whom happened to be Jayne Mansfield, at a Los Angeles benefit for our men in the service.

In 1966, trying to break out of the stereotype of being exclusively a kids' performer, I struck a deal with ABC and Ed Scherick, to star in a special, a comedy/variety which was also to feature Ernest Borgnine and Judy Garland, in what would have been her last television show appearance. We shot the show, but unfortunately, there was a shakeup at the network and Leonard Goldberg came in and he said he didn't want anything to do with it, so it was never aired (fortunately, I do have a taped copy of the show.) It's a wonderful show, with a great bit we did with Borgnine. It went like this: I introduce Judy Garland, and who comes onstage, singing his heart out, but Ernest Borgnine, trying to convince everyone that he's Judy Garland? Then, I join him, again playing Soupy to his Garland; we do a song, a dance—me as the man, Ernie as the woman—and then who should come out but Judy herself. It's a classic bit, one that I'm very sorry no one ever got to see, because, as I said, the network chose not to air it.

On the show, we also had another terrific, funny sketch called the "Great Explodo," which was a kind of forerunner of the Super Dave Osborne character that Bob Einstein (who, by the way, happens to be Albert Brooks's brother) did on his cable show, *Super Dave*, and a sketch with movie stars Joan Fontaine and Chester Morris that predated Woody Allen's *The Purple Rose of Cairo*. In it, I'm watching a film starring Chester and Joan and I step right into it and become a part of the movie.

SOUPY SEZ

Show me a woman who's misplaced her handbag and I'll show you a tote-all loss.

JIM REINA, TELEVISION PRODUCER:

I was the associate producer on Soupy's special, which meant that I was assisting Herb Sergeant, whom I knew from the old Steve Allen days. We actually worked together on the old *Tonight Show* in 1954, with Steve Allen. Anyway, he was doing this Soupy Sales special for ABC, with Dwight Hemion as the director—he did the Streisand specials—and he asked me to help him. Soupy's a great movie buff and the opening sequence, which was Soupy's idea and written, I think, with Herb's help, was brilliant. It had Soupy going into a film archive, he picks up an old movie, and suddenly he's in the midst of it. Actually, it was a film we made with Chester Morris and Joan Fontaine, which we shot up at some townhouse in the East Nineties. Funny thing about that, originally, Chester's costar was supposed to be an actress who shall remain nameless. Anyway, time comes for the shoot and she's nowhere to be found. She was staying at the Delmonico Hotel and they sent me down there to get her. I knocked on the door and there was no answer. Finally, I went downstairs and got the bellman and brought him up with me. He opens the door, we walk in, and there she is, dead drunk. I couldn't wake her and even if I could have, I knew she wouldn't be any good to us. So, I called up Herb and we started scurrying around, calling agents, looking for another actress who might be available. Finally, we wound up with Joan Fontaine. I remember, she didn't have the right clothes, so they sent me up to her place and her maid gave me a suitcase full of wardrobe to choose from.

There was a production number that Soupy did in the show. The music was *A Real Live Girl*, from the Broadway show, *Little Me*, with Sid Caesar. Soupy did it dancing with a bunch of chorus girls. I remember spending time in the rehearsal hall watching them. Soupy was terrific.

Then there was the classic bit with Ernest Borgnine as Judy Garland. As I remember, Ernest Borgnine was a good friend of Soupy's and they thought it would be a funny gag if they would introduce Judy and have Ernest come out instead. We were filming in a studio in Brooklyn and a couple of blocks away Sammy Davis Jr. was doing his show for NBC. I remember, we were shooting it and Herb, who was a man of few words, said, "Go next door and get Judy Garland to come over here."

"Are you kidding?"

"No," he said, "they know you're coming."

So, I went to the studio, got Judy, and escorted her back so she could do her cameo, and then I took her back to do the *Sammy Davis Show*.

Years later, I went to work at ABC, where I spent the last twenty years of my working life, and a guy who worked on programming said to me one day, "Hey, I just saw a show you worked on, and it was terrific." It was that Soupy Sales Special that never ran. All I know is that I heard that Leonard Goldberg, who came in as the head of programming,

With Franklin and Jimmy Roosevelt (the Mayor of Miami—wearing the white dinner jacket), during the filming of Birds Do It, *in Miami.*

said he didn't like it. He had the power to keep it off the air, so it just disappeared. And the thing is, it was very well produced, and they spent a lot of money on it. I worked on a lot of shows on NBC, and I have to say that it was one of the best shows I'd ever worked on.

. . .

Meanwhile, back at the ranch, we were still having trouble with Channel 5. They were so cheap they didn't want to budget anything for the "Philo Kvetch" bits, even though they were incredibly popular. Finally, I went to them and said, "Well, why don't you just give us so much money a week to budget? That way, we can save it up and use it when we need it." And that's what they did. They gave us the enormous sum of $100 a week, which was okay, I guess, until one week we wanted to do a particular sketch where there was going to be a giant horsefly and we were going to rig a big net. The bit was that I'd then come in with a big flyswatter to kill the giant horsefly. To produce this horsefly was going to cost us two hundred and fifty dollars. Of course, they said, "You can't do it."

"Why not?" I asked.

"It's over your budget," they said.

I did the bit anyway and sent them the bill for two hundred and fifty dollars. I don't know who paid it, but it wasn't me.

This fight over money, in fact fighting over every little thing, went on all the time and it was exhausting. I'm a pretty easygoing man, but it was a horrible ongoing battle that bothers me to this day.

One day, it was probably in late 1965, they actually came to me and said, "Do you want a raise?"

Well, I was supposed to get a raise, so I was, understandably, baffled by the question. "Certainly," I said.

"Well, you could turn it down," this particular executive said.

"No. I'm not going to turn it down," I said. "Why would I do that?" This conversation alone says something about those guys, doesn't it? These were weird people, the executives at WNEW. But as for the other people I worked with, the engineers, the cameramen, they were just beautiful. It was just those suits upstairs that drove me crazy.

FRANK NASTASI:

The executives at WNEW kept changing our time slot, and that hurts you because it makes it difficult for your audience to find when the show is on, as well as it tinkers with viewing habits. I think we were on as late as 6:30. And then at one point, they were pushing us back with the soap operas. This was Soupy's baby, but I got angry with the way they were treating us, so I said to Mel Bailey, one of the executives, "You can't compete with the soap operas. They're sacrosanct. You can't compete with them. Why are you putting us next to them?"

And Mel and the others said, "Well, that's why we're putting you close together. Because we figured you could compete with them."

What they didn't understand was that nobody, not even the pope, could compete with soap operas.

. . .

Peaches: Mr. Sales, will you marry me?
Soupy: No.
Peaches: Well, I just want you to know, when I get married a lot of men are going to be miserable.
Soupy: Well, how many men are you going to marry?

. . .

After the incredible success I had at the Paramount, we reached the height of our success—by 1966 we were syndicated in 50 television markets across the United States, as well as in Canada, New Zealand, and Australia. I had been a guest on *The Tonight Show* with Johnny Carson, *The Dean Martin Show*, *The Carol Burnett Show* and *The Bob Hope Show*. By that time, I had made something like 5,370 live television appearances, more than anyone else in the history of the medium.

I was, in short, the toast of New York. I don't know if it was rye or whole wheat, but it was fun. I had fallen in love with the city. It was the most exciting, stimulating place I'd ever been or seen, which is why I've made my home there and wouldn't think of living anywhere else. I especially enjoyed the music and nightlife—most of which is just a memory now—with clubs like the Copa and Danny's Hideaway, which were the big places in town. I went out as much as I could, in large part because I had to get away from the noise. Tony and Hunt, my future rock stars, had already started a band, called *Tony and the Tigers*, joined by the actor Burgess Meredith's son John, and by Jeff Alpert, whose father was a psychiatrist. Well, they practiced at home, so obviously there was no way of getting any peace. They actually put out a single called, "Summer Time (Is the Best Time for Making Love)." Tony and the Tigers appeared on *Hullaballoo* in 1966, when I was the host. They performed "Day Tripper," and later in the show, the Sales Brothers did a song-and-dance routine with me. It was a wonderful moment for me, one that I'll never forget. Today, both my boys are musicians. Tony lives in California, while Hunt resides in Austin, Texas.

My contract was up in September and in my mind, I just didn't want to sign up again. The fact is, I thought they had typecast me as being able to do only a kids' show, and I knew that I was more than that. And so, when the station came to me with a new contract, I turned them down.

FRANK NASTASI:

Many people think *The Soupy Sales Show* was canceled in 1966, but it wasn't. We walked out, or rather Soupy did. He got mad about something, I'm not sure what it was because he was mad all through the run of the show since the station was never giving us any help. Anyway, they got into a big argument, and I remember saying that I'd go up to see Mel Bailey the WNEW executive in charge at Channel 5, myself, even though that wasn't my duty. I remember saying, "Mel, don't you understand that you've got gold here?"

One comment was, and I think it was made by Mel Bailey, "Well, the fact is, the front office doesn't like to deal with personalities." Which was absolutely ridiculous.

I couldn't believe what I was hearing. I said, "You're always gonna deal with personalities!" That happened all the way back in the sixties, and look at me, I'm still getting mad now.

So, at one point, Soupy hit the wall and got really angry about something. A few of us walked into Soupy's office and pleaded with him, "Don't give up Soupy. Don't quit. That's what they want you to do. We've got something here. Let's not throw it away." You know, I was protecting my job, too, and Soupy understood that.

But he said, "I'm sorry, Frank, but I can't take it anymore." The whole thing was almost like a movie. The comedy, then the drama. The in-fighting with the executives. But we got along great with everybody else, as far as the cast and crew. And people were just dying to get on our show.

But Soupy was adamant. He just went up there and said, "I'm walking," and that was it. The show was over. And I couldn't get him to come back. He had the power then, and in the end, we figured we'd just find other jobs. And as for me, I got busy in the theater. But when I look back it makes me sad that those people just didn't know what they were doing, what they were losing. It was just stupid, is all.

It's amazing, but even today, what, thirty-five years later, I walk down the street and I'm getting recognized—I always say to a guy, one of my friends, "I wonder who's going to recognize me today." Certainly, Soupy's much more recognizable than I am, but still, even to be recognized as much as I am makes me feel good about it, about what we did and what we meant to people.

• • •

I think the show could have run quite a while. It was probably a combination of Soupy being tired of fighting with management and it was a constant struggle. I think what it goes back to is that the station didn't really recognize what they had.

—Art Seidel

• • •

There comes a time when you have to make a stand for what you think is right, and at the time I thought it was time to move on. I was tired of the constant struggle. I had faith in myself. I knew that I'd land on my feet. And so I quit. A lot of times you have to take stock of yourself, and that's what I did. I said to myself, "Look, I wouldn't have been in the business this long if I wasn't doing something right."

Me giving Frank advice on the set of Come Blow Your Horn.

Taken in front of the Keith-Albee theater for the 1966 world premier of Birds Do It. *My old Huntington friend, the beloved Burt Shemp, was the emcee. To my right is my mother, and that's Hunt in the foreground. Tony's face is hidden.*

A photo taken of me in Chicago at the Pheasant Run Theater in the early 1970s, or maybe it's a mug shot.

7

WHat's My Line?

NeW YORK 1966–1980

Soupy has always been a natural for a celebrity game show, because they're free form and put people in a perfect ad-lib situations. Soupy would give us not only a celebrity with the skill of playing the game, but also the persona of a very funny man. Someone like Soupy is much funnier than a straight actor, and besides being bright and good at all the games, Soupy always entertained.

—Bob Stewart, TV Show Game Producer

• • •

When I left my New York show in the fall of 1966, it was the first time in years I was able to do things beyond the little box that had been my home for so many years. For instance, in 1966 I had my first starring role in a film. It was called *Birds Do It*, and it's now shown in six states as capital punishment. I remember they sent me a script and I rejected it at first, because God knows you have to protect yourself in this business—people only blame who they see on screen, not the writers or directors. Actually, once it was rewritten, *Birds Do It* wasn't such a terrible picture. It was produced by Ivan

165

Tors, and if you ask me, I think it's where they got the idea for *The Flying Nun*. I played Melvin Bird, the janitor in a nuclear plant who gets accidentally "ionized," finds he can fly, and ends up capturing some spies. There were some good people in the cast, such as Tab Hunter (who'd also appeared on our New York TV show), the fine character actors Arthur O'Connell and Edward Andrews, and Doris Dowling, who had played a hooker opposite Ray Milland in *The Lost Weekend*.

I also had an offer from a new TV network—the United Network—to do a show from Las Vegas, but the network never got off the ground, so that didn't work out. What did get off the ground in 1967 was a starring role in a Broadway show called *Come Live with Me*, a farce that was written by Stanley Price and Lee Minoff, who was one of the screenwriters of the *Yellow Submarine* film. Unfortunately, unlike the Beatles' submarine, this sunk after only five performances. The problem was that the seats faced the stage. I portrayed Chuck Clark, a divorced American screenwriter in London who pretends he's still married just so he can hire Ingeborg, a beautiful live-in Danish au pair. Originally, the director was supposed to be Jonathan Miller, the English physician and man-about-the-theatre who'd made a big hit with Peter Cook and Dudley Moore in the brilliant revue *Beyond the Fringe*. One newspaper did a piece on the show and made a point of our unlikely collaboration, comparing it to Olivier working with Jerry Lewis, or Michelangelo Antonioni directing an episode of *Hogan's Heroes*. As it turned out, Miller spent most of his time on the phone with Jackie Kennedy—he was a real name-dropper—and he left the show during rehearsals and was replaced by Joshua Shelley. The opening night critics destroyed us. The *New York Times'* Walter Kerr, the most powerful reviewer in town, said something like, "Now that we've met Soupy Sales, it would be nice to see him in a play," which I thought was pretty nasty. Later, we got a very favorable write-up in *The New Yorker* as well as in *The Saturday Review* and *Cue*, but it was too late. Nevertheless, we took the play on the road and played to packed houses in states like Florida and Michigan. We always got great laughs and did good business, so I guess it was a play after all.

Of course, we had our share of mishaps. One night, for instance, I went to open a door onstage and the doorknob came off in my hand and flew out into the audience. Some old guy caught it. I went up to him and said, "Sir, if we don't get this doorknob back, we'll be in this house all night long." Another night, I was supposed to fall back and another actor was supposed to catch me, but when I fell, his knee hit me in the back and I was sore for a week.

This sobering Broadway experience led to my next gig, a revival of the old *Hellzapoppin'*, which was a bunch of skits loosely tied together. We performed it at the World's Fair: Montreal's Expo '67, and we played two shows a day, seven days a week, and I enjoyed it quite a bit, partly because I got to write a lot of the material myself. It was here that I ran into that gorgeous dancer who had graced the nation with her rendition of the Mouse a few years earlier on the *Ed Sullivan Show*. Yes, Trudy Carson was a member of the cast of *Hellzapoppin'* and, as I said earlier, it was this meeting that would begin our relationship, but it wouldn't be until twelve years later that we would actually be married, because, even though I was separated from my wife, it would take that long to get our divorce.

TRUDY CARSON SALES:

After our meeting at the *Ed Sullivan Show*, I didn't see Soupy again for two years, during which time I did a couple of Broadway shows, *I Had a Ball* and *Skyscraper*, as well as an industrial film. I missed the Equity call for *Hellzapoppin'* because I was cast in the ill-fated *Breakfast at Tiffany's* on Broadway with Mary Tyler Moore and Richard Chamberlain, which closed before it opened, and that was when the stage manager, Jerry Adler [Adler is now an actor who has appeared in many popular television programs like *The Sopranos*], called me in for a private audition for *Hellzapoppin'*, which was the show that Soupy was going to star in. Jerry remembered me from *I Had a Ball*, where he had the same job—and that's how I was called in for a part.

I didn't make the first day of rehearsal because I was doing the Kraft Music Hall and came in the next morning with only a couple of hours of sleep. Soupy remembered me from the Sullivan show—or at least he said he did.

Anyway, I got the job and it was a wild experience. We did two shows a night, seven nights a week, for three months. I wasn't in any

What's My
Line? *Joanna
Barnes, host,
Wally Brunner,
Alan Alda, and
Arlene Francis.*

*$50,000 Pyramid,
1981, with Dick
Clark, and the
winner. Notice me
trying to hold
onto that check.*

scenes with Soupy, except that I was an understudy to one of the principals who, near the end of the run, hurt her foot, and so I did have to go on stage with him.

Actually, I had been engaged to someone else for four years at the time I went to do *Hellzapoppin'*. I remember we were playing the World's Fair in Montreal and there were two ways to get to the theater, either by driving or by taking the ferry. One day, I was taking the ferry, sitting next to another dancer, and Soupy got on. We caught each other's eyes and they locked and the entire trip, we never took our eyes off each other. Later, I thought about how awkward it must have been and how rude we were to that poor girl sitting between us. It was like we were paralyzed, or at least I was, bewitched, barely able to speak or move. When we stepped off of that ferry, we went our separate ways, but I could not forget that moment that eventually had so much to do with changing my life. It hit me when I wasn't even looking. By "it" I mean "it," and this was really "IT." Period.

When we got back to New York and Soupy became separated from his wife, he called me. It didn't surprise me, of course. We had a very long courtship—we were married in 1980. During those years, I continued my career, appearing in the original cast of *Follies*; *Irene*, with Debbie Reynolds; *New Faces of '68*; the film *All That Jazz*; and several industrial films and TV shows.

During our courtship, Soupy was very romantic. He wrote me love letters. He would write them on a napkin and I saved them in a huge plastic bag.

• • •

In 1968 I got a call that was to send me right back to television, but in a totally unexpected role, propelling me into a new career in the 1970s and on into the 1980s as a TV game show panelist.

The call was an offer to be a panelist on *What's My Line?*, the old quiz show from the '50s which had gone back into syndication and aired on Sunday nights on CBS, with Wally Bruner as the host. I was booked only for one week, but I guess I impressed them with my ability to ad-lib, so they signed me to be a regular on the show, along with Arlene Francis, with rotating guest panelists taking the other two spots.

For the next seven years, I was a regular on *What's My Line?*, racking up a total of fifteen hundred segments, first with Wally Bruner as the host and later, Larry Blyden, whose tragic death in a car accident just before his fiftieth birthday ended the program.

It was a wonderful time for me. I was following in the footsteps of intellectual giants and game show experts like Bennett Cerf and Dorothy Kilgallen. We would do five shows in one day, and I didn't have to go on the road and, better yet, I was making pretty good money. Of course, there were some drawbacks. Despite the fact that I was still doing my standup act, I found that I missed the daily grind of doing my own show, because I didn't have that creative outlet.

But of all the game shows I did over the years, *What's My Line?* was my favorite because it gave me the opportunity to show that I was more than just a kids' entertainer, plus it gave me the chance to ad-lib. And I have to say that I was pretty good at figuring out people's professions.

I also appeared on *Match Game, Beat the Clock,* and the *$20,000 Pyramid,* (later that figure was bumped up several times—inflation's a bitch, isn't it?), where I won more money for contestants than anyone else in the history of the show. Mark Goodson and Bill Todman were beautiful for me—they were experienced and knew how to run a ship.

As a result of my appearances on these game shows, I think the public's perception of me changed over this period, as my ability to answer questions on a range of topics demonstrated that I had more on the ball than the nutcase I portrayed on my show. I loved *Pyramid*, not only because it gave me the opportunity to use my mind and entertain folks, but also because it ran fifteen years and put plenty of bread on the table.

BOB STEWART, TV GAME SHOW PRODUCER, "PASSWORD" AND "$25,000 PYRAMID":

I used Soupy on almost every other game show I ever produced. And whenever I tried out a new show, I used Soupy. The way it worked was like this: I would go to a network executive and submit an oral presentation. If they liked it, I'd be asked to do a run-through. Sometimes we'd have a small audience and sometimes we'd just have an audience of executives. We would gather some celebrities and go into an informal setting and show them a brand new game. Under those circumstances Soupy was a tremendous asset because of his natural ability to not only get into the game, but also to respond to any situation around him in a way that will invariably entertain the audience. He always brought such great enthusiasm and originality to any show that we did.

The *Pyramid* show was on for eighteen years, from 1973 to 1992, and during that time we would cycle our celebrities. When we were filming in New York, Soupy was one of the regulars that we would rotate, and even when we moved out to L.A. to do the shows, we would go to the trouble of flying him out, just because he was so good at what we needed—the ability to play the game and the ability to entertain the audience.

On the *Pyramid*, we would have two teams, each team headed by a celebrity, and the only pattern that was important to us on the show as to the celebrities we booked was that we wanted our competitors to be on equal footing as far as skills were concerned. In that respect, we put Soupy in the top ranks of players, and we'd have to pair him up with a female who was also in that top rank, women like Lynn Redgrave, Betsy Palmer, and Anita Gillette. The reason we did that was to make sure it was a competitive game.

We would tape five shows a day, and have a lunch break after the second show. During that break, there'd be ten or twelve of us sitting around the table, celebrities and the production staff, and even during lunchtime Soupy would put on a show for us.

I remember one time we were in the studio taping the show—Soupy was not working with us at that particular time. We broke for lunch and we were sitting around, I believe William Shatner was one of the celebrity guests on that series of shows—and I thought of a story Soupy had told me a couple of weeks before that was hysterical. I started to try to tell the story but before I got very far I realized that there was no way I could do any justice to it, so I said, "Listen, I'm gonna call Soupy and ask him to come over and tell the story." So, I pick up the phone and I get Soupy, and I say, "Soupy, I'm sitting here with William Shatner and the production crew and I want to tell them that story you told me a couple of weeks ago, but there's no way I can do it properly, so would you mind coming over and telling them the story?"

And without missing a beat, Soupy said, "Bob, go fuck yourself." I fell on the floor laughing.

Here's another side of Soupy that most people don't know about. When Soupy's fiftieth birthday came around, his wife, Trudy, called me and said, "Bob, we're having a party for Soupy at our apartment, and we'd love for you and Anne Marie," that's my wife, "to come over and celebrate with us." We said yes, of course, and we got there on a Saturday night around 7 o'clock. There was no one there and I figured, well, we're the first to arrive. So we sat there and had drinks and hors d'oeurves, and suddenly I realized that the evening was getting later and later and Trudy was in the kitchen cooking, and no one else had come. By eight-thirty it finally dawned on me that the four of us were celebrating Soupy's fiftieth birthday. Now, what was interesting to me was that wherever Soupy is, he's the center of attention and so my idea of a fiftieth birthday party was a big blast with a hundred people. Now don't get me wrong, it was hardly New Year's Eve, but I was having a very good time. It's just that I thought we'd have a mob here. When I mentioned this to Trudy, she said, "In his private moments Soupy's not comfortable with a lot of people, but he's comfortable with you guys." I was complimented, but it surprised me. I never forgot that evening— not only because we had a great time and Trudy's a wonderful cook, but because I always remembered my surprise at the intimacy of it.

• • •

Back in the late 1960s, my friend and game show boss Bob Stewart approached me and asked if I'd be willing to appear on a new game show that he was developing. He called it *Personality* and it had a very interesting premise. The idea was that Bob and his staff would take a celebrity and ask him or her all kinds of odd, eccentric, thought-provoking questions. Then, they'd take those answers and go to another group of celebrities, tell them who the original celebrity who did the interview was and, giving them several choices, ask them what answers they thought that celebrity gave to the questions. Larry Blyden, who was also doing *What's My Line?* at the time, was the host of the show and it was taped in New York's Rockefeller Center.

Recently, Bob, in going through his files, found a transcript of my original sessions and, in looking over some of my answers, I was surprised, embarrassed, and occasionally pleased at what I said. I thought it might be interesting to give you a few examples of the questions and my answers, so here goes (and remember, my answers were totally spontaneous—we had no time to prepare a witty or insightful reply:)

```
FINISH THESE PHRASES:

Bob: When I put on theatrical make up I. . .
Soupy: I'm happy.
Bob: Every human being is entitled to . . .
Soupy: A couple of mistakes.
Bob: I learned the hard way that . . .
Soupy: That you can take nothing for granted.
Bob: Men who cheat . . .
Soupy: Shouldn't play solitaire.
Bob: Man's greatest weakness is . . .
Soupy: His inability to deal with women.
Bob: The trouble with women is . . .
Soupy: Men.
Bob: The only way to make yourself understood by
     a woman is . . .
Soupy: To explain it very slowly.
Bob: Show me a successful man and I'll show
     you . . .
Soupy: A woman in back of him . . . nagging.
Bob: A woman is entitled to alimony if . . .
Soupy: If she's got a better lawyer than her husband.
Bob: If I had it to do over again . . .
Soupy: I'd hope that I would have done it better.


ANSWER THESE QUESTIONS IN ONE SENTENCE OR LESS:

Bob: Can you think of one fact of life that you
     really don't like to live with?
```

Soupy: I guess that maybe there's the possibility that you might fail at something.

Bob: What can bring a smile to your face quicker than anything else?

Soupy: Another person's smile.

Bob: What in life was the thing that was most difficult for you to achieve?

Soupy: I imagine it was regaining the companionship and the love of the rest of my family.

Bob: What is the one thing you can't resist?

Soupy: Hot dogs.

Bob: What's the best line of advice you ever received?

Soupy: Not to pay any attention to what people say about you.

Bob: What's the best piece of advice you ever received about sex?

Soupy: "Don't talk to the blonde waitress down at the corner restaurant." No, no. It was, "Read a Sears-Roebuck catalogue, because you have to get through the women's lingerie to get to the toy section."

Bob: How do you think a woman can make a fool out of a man?

Soupy: I think the mere idea that she's a woman can make a fool out of a man.

Bob: What do you think is the quality that most women hope for in a husband?

Soupy: That he would be rich, deaf, dumb, blind, own a liquor store, and drive a Rolls Royce.

Bob: If you were going to be locked in a room for six months or a year and to keep you company you could only have the sound of one other thing, what would it be?

Soupy: A Count Basie album.

Bob: And if in that room you were permitted to hang one thing on the wall to keep you company for a year, what would it be?

Soupy: A mirror. And being two-faced I could kiss me.

Bob: If you could be one instrument, what would it be?

Soupy: Gee, I don't know. If you're a piano, people would be saying that you should go on a diet.

Bob: When you watch yourself on the screen, whether it be television or motion pictures, how do you react to yourself?

Soupy: Well, I go in with the idea of liking it, but I usually cover my eyes and sort of look up and sort of slump down in my seat.

Bob: If reincarnation were a possibility and you were going to come back, how would you like to come back?

Soupy: As a dog. A French poodle.

Bob: How are you most different from your public image?

Soupy: Well, I guess I'm probably like a lot of other people—I have my depressed moments.

Bob: If you were in front of an audience about to take one turn at Russian Roulette, before you pulled that trigger, what would you say?

Soupy: Well, I guess I'd look out into the audience and I'd say, "Anybody got any calamine lotion? 'Cause I've got an itchy trigger finger."

Bob: If you could live your life over again, is there anything you'd not do again?

Soupy: Well, I know one thing I would do, live it over a delicatessen. But no, if I had my life to live over again I wouldn't have signed with the William Morris Agency.

Bob: Can you think of something that success has taken from you?

Soupy: It hasn't taken anything from me, but it's brought me a whole new class of enemies.

Bob: Is there any song title or song lyric that seems to express your philosophy or your feeling about life?

Soupy: I guess it would be, "Day in, day out . . ."

Bob: If you could have your name as author of anything that has been done in the past, a novel, a song, a musical comedy, a work of nonfiction, what would you have liked to have written?

Soupy: The song "Stardust."

Bob: If you were an English nobleman and you had a coat of arms, considering your life and the kind of man you are, how would you describe it?

Soupy: It would probably read, "The last one in is a rotten egg."

Bob: If you had to wear a button in your lapel with a permanent message on it, what would it be?

Soupy: "Always play it cool, never lose your enthusiasm, and the world is yours."

Bob: What do you think about when you're looking at yourself while shaving in the morning?

Soupy: I wonder whether I should have gotten out of bed in the first place.

Bob: In what respect do you think you're still a pretty old-fashioned guy?

Soupy: When it comes to drinking Old Fashioneds.
Actually, I'm an old-fashioned guy when it
comes to old-fashioned girls.

Bob: If you'd been born a woman, what kind of
woman do you think you'd have been?

Soupy: The ugliest broad in the United States.

Bob: What if you woke up tomorrow and found out
that you were the last man in a world
filled with women. What would you do?

Soupy: I'd have the locks removed from my doors.

Bob: What do you think men over forty are most
concerned about?

Soupy: Looking like they were thirty.

Bob: What's the one thing that makes you furi-
ous?

Soupy: That some people who are supposed to be
doing their job aren't doing it.

Bob: What's the one habit you can't seem to
break?

Soupy: I think it's probably trusting a lot of
people.

Bob: What would you do if you were offered a book
that would tell your future?

Soupy: I wouldn't open it. I don't want to read about
it. I'd want to be there when it happens.

Bob: What would the title of a book about your
life be?

Soupy: "To Have and Have Not."

Bob: What one line in the English language is the
most important or the most impressive line
to you?

Soupy: I think the line that always impressed me
most was something Damon Runyon once said,
and that is, "You're only here for a short
while, so take time to smell the flowers."

Bob: How do you react when your birthday rolls around?

Soupy: Well, I'm another day older and deeper in debt.

Bob: When you open a newspaper, what section do you turn to first?

Soupy: The obituaries. If my name isn't in it, I shave.

Bob: Is there any fate that you could think of which would be regarded as a fate worse than death?

Soupy: Yeah, that would be, you're the last man on Earth and you jump off a building and as you're sailing past the forty-fourth floor you hear the phone ring.

Bob: What one thing has to happen in the course of a day to make it good or perfect for you?

Soupy: To be able to get up and read the obituary section and find that my name isn't in it.

Bob: If you were asked to improvise your own epitaph, how do you think it would read?

Soupy: With my luck they wouldn't have enough money for a headstone and they'd have to bury me up to my neck. But if I did have to write my own epitaph I guess I'd like it to say, "He was a nice guy."

• • •

In 1968, I was performing at a roast of the Smothers Brothers at a midtown restaurant. The vice president of CBS happened to be there, and after the roast was over he took me aside and said, "Soupy, I want to talk to you about something."

"Yeah," I said—you see, I'll talk to anybody, even if they are a network executive.

"We're thinking of doing a special with the Harlem Globetrotters and I wondered if you'd be interested."

"Sure," I said, never missing an opportunity to work with guys who are taller than I am.

I went home and thought about it for a while, and finally came up with an idea that I thought might work: the Globetrotters were looking for a coach and I'd be sweeping up the courts one day and a ball would come over to me and I'd throw it up toward the basket and sink it. You can figure out the rest. I thought it was a pretty funny concept, and they did too, so they sent me to Atlantic City, where the Globetrotters were getting ready to make an appearance.

I got out there on the court during practice and, standing at half-court, among all these legendary ballplayers like Meadowlark Lemon and Curly Neale, and I launched the ball up in the air in the general direction of the basket and sure enough, swish! right through the hoop. They couldn't believe it. (And, frankly, neither could I.) "Ah, you'll never do that again," they taunted me, so, I threw up another shot and would you believe it, swish! Right through the hoop again. It was wild.

Anyway, despite being shown up by a short white guy, the Globetrotters loved my idea, and we wound up shooting the special at Madison Square Garden and, wouldn't you know it, I must have tried that shot from half-court a hundred times and not one of them went in. Finally, they just had to do a bit of television magic, otherwise known as trick photography, compliments of tape editing, to make it go through the hoop.

There is a postscript to this story. My manager, Stan Greeson, would end up becoming President of the Globetrotters and eventually they got their own show and—would you believe it?—they never ever had me on the show.

• • •

During the 1970s, I made numerous appearances on the highly rated and very popular syndicated *Mike Douglas Show*, from Philadelphia, including many, many stints as his guest cohost. Mike had a combination variety/talk show that was on in the late afternoons in most venues. We did all kinds of wacky stunts, including me being thrown into a giant pie, but after a while I grew to dislike Mike because of something he did.

The Mike Douglas Show, *with Mike on right, and Moe Howard checking me out as a potential fourth stooge.*

It got to me that Mike had heard somewhere, I don't know where, that I had spoken to a producer and told him not to use Mike in a film. Totally untrue. But Mike believed it and stopped using me on his show. I got wind of this and confronted him. "Mike," I said, "why would I ever do something like that? Why would I care if so and so used you in a movie. It's ridiculous." I don't know if he believed me or not, but I guess he didn't, because he never used me on his show again. But what really pissed me off was that when his book came out a few years ago, he went on all these talk shows and constantly showed clips of me on his show, hitting people with pies, getting hit with pies . . . and the funny thing was, not once did he ever mention me in his book.

During this period, I also appeared in a few films, including *Critic's Choice,* with Bob Hope (one of my idols growing up), and *Don't Push, I'll Change When I'm Ready,* with Sue Lyon, Duane Hickman, and Cesar Romero, both in 1970.

For *Critic's Choice,* Bob called me one day and asked me if I'd appear in the film with him. At the time, I was pretty hot and I didn't want to do a small role in a film and have them advertise it as a Soupy Sales film, so I said, "Sure, just so long as you don't credit me." So, in an uncredited cameo performance, I played a hotel desk clerk. It was fun and I loved Bob and worked with him on a few other occasions. It was quite a kick working with someone I'd stolen routines from when I was a kid starting out—but don't tell Bob that.

I also went on the road with my nightclub act, working with singers like Patti Page, Steve Lawrence, and Edye Gorme. I still managed to fit in appearances in a few TV shows, like *Love, American Style.* I costarred twice on *Love*—once as the husband to Stephanie Powers, and another time when I played an angel who came down on Christmas Eve to cheer up Sam Jaffe, who'd lost his wife. In 1975, I hosted a Saturday morning show for kids called *Almost Anything Goes,* in which teams of kids would compete against each other for prizes that would go to their schools. I loved working with the kids and I loved it when they were able to win something for their schools.

You know me by now—anything to keep me busy and off the streets. But seriously, as you've probably figured out by now, I thrive on work. It's not just the attention I get, although that's not bad, it's just that I need to keep working in order to feel alive.

. . .

A lot of strange, wacky things have happened to me over the years, but one that I'll probably never forget involved a famous gangster and one of the greatest comedians/straight men of all time.

It was 1973 and George Burns and I were attending the funeral service for the comic genius, Joe E. Lewis, which was being held at the legendary Frank E. Campbell funeral home on the upper east side of Manhattan. George and I went inside and found a couple of seats and when we sat down we noticed that the two seats next to us were taped off, as if they were reserved.

I turned to George and said, "Hey, George, I wonder who these seats are reserved for?"

"I don't know, Soupy, but it must be for someone pretty important."

So, we're sitting there and suddenly in walks these two guys, headed toward the seats. One of them is a fellow named Bill Rosen, who I knew as owning a bunch of restaurants in Los Angeles, and the guy next to him was none other than Frank Costello, the gangster who was one of the highest-ranking members of the Mafia.

The two guys sit down next to us and Costello looks over at me and says, "Soupy Sales. I love you. You're one of my favorites!" and he sticks out his hand to shake mine.

"Thank you," I say, and the truth was, I kinda couldn't believe it. Frank Costello. A fan of mine? It was exciting.

Anyway, George Burns leans over to me and says, only kinda half-whispers, "Ask him if he's carrying a gun."

And Frank Costello looks at me and says, "What did George say?"

Without missing a beat, I come back and say, "This isn't any fun." And he says, "No, it isn't." George won't let up. Now he says to me, "Ask him if he's gonna kill anybody." Frank Costello, still leaning on every word, shoots back with, "What did George just say?" Again without missing a beat, I say, "This isn't a thrill for anybody." Costello says, "He's right."

And then before George can say anything else, I turn to him and whisper "Cool it, George—you're gonna get us killed."

Fortunately, that was the end of it, but don't think I didn't sit there the rest of the service hoping that all those gunshots Costello had heard might have affected his hearing.

Clyde Adler and me on the Mike Douglas Show, 1970s.

Junior Almost Anything Goes, late 1970s.

. . .

When the early 1970s arrived and I finished appearing in *Hellzapoppin'*, I decided that I would create a nightclub act and perform at various clubs around the country. I loved the idea of performing live in front of my fans on a more intimate basis. And so, I incorporated some of the stuff I was doing on television, along with a standup routine—just like the old days back in Huntington—and a few songs. Over the years, I would hone the act, but I never pretended it was anything more than it was—just the ol' Soup doin' his thing. Paul Dver, whom I'd met when he was a kid working at NBC, was my accompanist.

PaUL DVER, SOUPY'S LONGTIME MUSICAL DIRECTOR AND ACCOMPANIST:

It was around 1974 or '75 and I was appearing in a version of a Neil Simon play, *Star Spangled Girl*, which Soupy had done at one time. We did it at Theatre for the New City, down in the East Village, and Soupy came down and saw me in the play. Two years later I get a call from Soupy and he says "All right, Paul, I've got a gig in Lodi, New Jersey. How about you come over there with me?"

This was something I will never forget, because I was so nervous. He came over and he gave me all his music and we rehearsed. I just did everything he wanted me to do. I learned all the piano parts, and I learned what he wanted me to say to him during the show.

I invited everybody who knew me to come out to Lodi, New Jersey, and see this show. I remember the guy who picked us up was a nice guy, but he had a little coordination problem; I think maybe he was like a little spastic. He kept twitching and hitting the wheel of the car on the way out. I'll never forget it. He was going, "Soupy, it's great to see you!" Bang on the wheel. At first, I thought it was just him being enthusiastic, but then he went "So how long are you going to be?" Bangs on the wheel. Soupy was sitting in the front seat, and he turned to me and he gives me this look that says, "Holy Shit. This guy's gonna drive us?" And meanwhile, I'm in the back seat hysterical. But that was just a hint as to whul kind of night it was going to be.

I got out there for the first show and right away I see they don't have a piano, they have an organ. Now, I can play a small organ, but this wasn't that; this was a giant church-type organ with pedals. When I saw it I said, "Soupy, I don't play these things."

He turned to the guy and said, "I told you, we needed a piano."

The guy just shrugged and said, "Well, we've got the organ and that's all we've got." So, ostensibly, everybody came to see my first show with Soupy and heard me go, "daaahhh-daaahhh-daaahhh"—because that's pretty much all I was able to do the whole night. Soupy would tell a joke and I'd go, "da-nah" on the organ. Whenever I tried to play something the least bit more complicated, it just sounded like Radio City Music Hall. "Da nah na na." Totally out of character for the act. So, that kind of set the tone for the evening.

In the meantime, Soupy did pretty much a solo thing and you know, he let me do my "da na". He didn't mind—but he certainly wasn't happy with the level of the gig we were doing. But it was kind of prophetic: It was our first time together, and it was like, "If you can make it through this, you've got a chance."

Soup did call me again a couple of months later to go with him on a gig and, after we performed together a few times (with a piano!), it started to get good. As a performer, I would start to insert ideas I had as to what I could do. And I knew it worked if Soupy didn't say anything. If he objected to anything by saying specifically, "Don't do that," after a show, I would just stop it. But generally, he would say to me, "Why didn't you do the so and so like you did last time?"

I'd say, "Well, you never said anything."

And he'd say, "No, it's in. It's in." And so I knew, if Soupy said something, it was out, and if he didn't say something, he expected it next time.

It was like this for about two years, and it started getting good. Soupy would get booked in some resorts and clubs in the Catskills, or with audiences that weren't the typical Soupy fans since they were already old when he started his career, but still the act started to play. People started to get off on our interplay together. In 1977, Soupy was booked into the glamorous Rainbow Grill at Rockefeller Center, and he said to me, "OK, this is it. Everybody's going to cover it. This is my debut."

I was really surprised, because you're talking about a big star in television and here he is excited that he's going to have his big New York nightclub debut. It was really kind of sweet.

Of course he was right. All the TV stations were covering the opening. There were announcements like, "Soupy Sales is opening tonight at the Rainbow Grill." And they put posters all around New York with our names on them.

That night went fantastic! Fantastic. Earl Wilson who was a columnist for the *New York Post* at the time wrote, "Soupy Sales has arrived." And everybody—every paper—raved at what an amazing act he put on. Suddenly, we were being booked all over. At that time, HBO was starting out and they were doing the on-location comedy acts. Robert Klein did the first, and then there was George Carlin, and then a few others. We were booked in 1978 at The Comedy Store, Mitzi Shore's place in California, and that's where HBO taped us. At the time, this was in 1978, I was twenty-three, and I was going all around the country, accompanying Soupy while he was making all these appearances.

Soupy wanted to have the show locked in. You can't do a nightclub act—nobody, even the Rat Pack, does a nightclub act that's free form. But he made it appear as if it were free form. Soupy was incredibly fast on his feet, and that's from his experiences on live television. In fact, I used to enjoy watching his ability to ad-lib when things did not quite go as planned. I would sometimes literally fall off the piano bench laughing at the way Soupy handled the unforeseen twists in the show.

I was supposed to hit Tiger Woods with a pie,
but the wrong tiger came out of the woods!

8

CALIFORNIA, HERE I COME...AGAIN!

LOS ANGELES, 1978

You can lead a horse to water, but if you can get him to float on his back, you've really got something.

· · ·

In 1978, I came back to television on a more regular basis, as a costar on *Sha-Na-Na*'s syndicated series. It whet my appetite for a regular gig, and so a year later, when the opportunity arose, I returned to Los Angeles to do what turned out to be ninety episodes of *The New Soupy Sales Show*. The plan was to incorporate most of the features of the old *Soupy Sales Show*—White Fang, Black Tooth, Pookie, Peaches, the Words of Wisdom, and, of course, pies and lots of 'em and, get this gang, I'd actually be in color. At the same time, we were hoping to update the show to keep it "hip." We taped an incredible six shows in two days each week.

Unfortunately, the problem was that it was marketed as simply as a kids' show and it wasn't. And so, once again, I was typecast and, as a result, the show didn't last anywhere near as long as it should have. Nevertheless, I'm very proud of what we did.

. . .

a SOUPY MEMORY FROM MARK EVANIER:

For about a year, back in the 1950s, my life revolved around a rubbery-faced little man who lived on a television soundstage with even rubberier house pets. His name was Soupy Sales and his pets were White Fang, Black Tooth, Pookie, and Hippy. I felt like part of the family, even though I was the only one who didn't periodically smash him in the face with a shaving-cream pie. The jokes were not new: some had doubtlessly been heckled at the Parthenon. And, just to make certain surprise was kept to a minimum, Soupy repeated material over and over and over. Still, it only added to the appeal that I could sit there and (usually) figure out where a joke was going before the inevitable punch line, followed by the inviolate pie-in-the-puss, always accompanied by a rifle shot sound effect. For kids—for adults even—there is a joy of the expected and a special pride to be one step ahead of those folks on the TV.

Lunch with Soupy Sales consisted of Soupy, his four pets, and an endless array of people who came to the door to annoy him, exploit him, and, invariably, pie him. All the people at the door and all four pets were performed by Clyde Adler, who was the perfect straight man for the Sales madness. As I learned from newspaper articles of the time, Adler was not a professional comedian; he was, by trade, a film editor at the Detroit TV station where Soupy had invented his winning format. Conscripted to help Soupy there, he had taken an open-ended sabbatical from the editing biz to migrate West with the comic. Clyde played White Fang and Black Tooth, then raced around to the back of the set to play Pookie or Hippy or some guy at the door. Except for the rarest of accidents, no part of him but his voice and forearms ever appeared on the show. Sometimes, Pookie and Hippy would fill three minutes, miming to a scratchy record by Stan Freberg, Johnny Standley, or Eddie "The Old Philsopher" Lawrence. And at the end would come the pie. Always the pie.

The format was wonderful . . . and I wasn't the only one who felt that way. Soupy, before he upped and moved his operation to New York, was the hero of every kid my age in L.A. (and quite a few kids my parents' ages). Oddly enough, though every boy I knew wanted to grow up to be Soupy, that was never my fantasy. When we ripped him off and did Soupy's show in the schoolyard, I was the only one who wanted to be Clyde Adler—not the star but the guy behind the scenes. And, if truth be known, what I *really* wanted to be one of those people you heard laughing in the background . . . someone who was part of that wonderful world, who'd had a hand in making it all happen. I didn't realize it at the time, but what I really wanted to be was Soupy's writer. I don't think he had one at the time but, if he did, that's what I would have wanted to be.

When folks ask me how it was I became a writer—at times, a professional comedy writer—I cannot answer truthfully without telling them about Soupy. If they remember the show—and most people do—they understand fully about wanting to be one of those guys you heard laughing behind the camera.

Soupy was finally canceled and Clyde Adler went back to editing film in Detroit. A year or three later, Soupy took New York TV by storm with a new show—the same show he'd done out here but with Frank Nastasi taking Clyde's roles. It was probably as good a show as he'd done in L.A., but I never got the chance to see it. A whole generation of kids on the East Coast, however, grew up with the same devotion my friends and I had known in our Soupy days.

In 1978, I was hired as head writer of an NBC variety pilot called *Anson 'n' Lorrie*, starring Anson Williams (then costar of TV's number one series, *Happy Days*) and his then newlywed bride, Lorrie Mahaffey. Fred Silverman was running NBC, and he had a hunch that this duo could combine the best qualities of Sonny and Cher and/or Donnie and Marie, two of his more notable past successes. We hired some good guest stars (Ron Hoard, Eddie Rabbitt, Gary Coleman, Al Molinaro) and a band of comedy sketch players (Jeff Altman, Darrow Igus, Louise DuArt, and Anna Mathias) and checked into KTLA Studios in Hollywood to tape us a pilot. KTLA is a local station (Channel 5 in Los Angeles) but its main business is renting its huge facilities to TV production companies. Their lot was once Warner Brothers' Hollywood facility. Stage 6, where we did *Anson 'n' Lorrie*, was where Al Jolson filmed *The Jazz Singer*. The small building that KTLA used for its newsroom offices was, once upon a time, the home of Leon Schlesinger's cartoon studio (i.e., the birthplace of Bugs Bunny). *WKRP in Cincinnati* taped on Stage 3, and other shows—network and syndication—were sprinkled across the lot.

Our first day there, I ran into Perry Cross, a producer I knew. He asked me what I was doing and I told him. Then I asked him what he was doing and he said, "Oh, I'm doing the new *Soupy Sales Show*." I did a take that Tex Avery would have considered overacting.

"What new *Soupy Sales Show*?"

Perry took me by the wrist, led me eight steps through a studio door, and I was suddenly standing on the set, watching Soupy Sales rehearsing a dance number. "*This* new *Soupy Sales Show*," said Perry.

Soupy was doing a new, syndicated version of his Soupy classic program, he explained. "With White Fang and Black Tooth and Pookie and Hippy?" I asked.

"With White Fang and Black Tooth and Pookie and Hippy," he proudly confirmed.

"Who's doing them?" I asked. My instant assumption was that they'd either hired someone new or imported Frank Nastasi from New York . . . which was a shame. Now that I was this close to one of my childhood fantasies, one piece—Clyde Adler—was probably missing.

"We got the guy who worked with Soupy in Detroit and L.A.," Perry proudly announced. "Clyde Adler."

I probably had the stupidest, most demented grin on my face. I have one right now, as I think about that moment—and all the moments before, watching Soupy and Clyde, listening to the crew laughing in the background, wishing I could be there. Suddenly, I *was* there. I told Perry just enough of this to not sound like a total ninny.

"Would it be okay," I asked, "if I kind of hung around when you're taping? I won't get in the way."

"If it's okay with the director, it's okay with me," Perry said. Just then, the director wandered up and, continuing this cavalcade of coincidences, it turned out to be Lou Horvitz, a charming gent I knew from a recent, abortive project. (I know it sounds here like I know everyone in

Hollywood, but I don't now and I knew even fewer then; it was maybe a one-in-a-hundred coincidence that Soupy's new show was being produced and directed by two acquaintances.)

Lou said it was fine with him if I loitered on their set. "Anytime you want, Mark," he said. But just as quickly, he broke my heart by turning to Perry and saying, "Geez, we should've hired Mark as one of the writers."

"Yeah," Perry said. "Now you think of it . . . when it's too late." Oh, the pain, the pain. But at least I had the run of the place. I got to meet Soupy and Clyde and to watch them taping and to be one of those folks in the background laughing on the adjoining stage, at the jokes. For the next few weeks, while we rehearsed and taped our show I commuted between tapings, alternately playing audience and head writer.

Though the *Anson 'n' Lorrie* pilot had five times the prestige (and, probably, ten times the salary), there was no doubt in my mind which of the shows I'd rather have worked on.

The producer of *Anson 'n' Lorrie* was a bright lady named Bonny Dore who, like Soupy and Clyde, hailed from Detroit. In fact, she'd gotten her start in television at the Detroit ABC affiliate and had once mentioned to me that she had been friends with both gents, Clyde especially. I arranged a lunch with Clyde for the three of us.

The next morning, Bonny and I were locked in for several hours working on the rundown for the show. I steadfastly refused to tell her who we were lunching with until, around noon, a call came in for us and I put it on the speaker-phone.

"Hello?" I said.

Over the speaker came the unmistakable tones of White Fang: "Raah-oh-raah-oh-raah!"

In my best Soupy-style, I decoded: "Oh, hi, White Fang! You say you want to have lunch today?"

"Raah-oh-raah!"

"Fine," I said. "Can you be ready at 12:30?"

"Uh-ruh."

"Well then, how about one o'clock?"

"Raah!"

"Okay, we'll swing by Stage 2 for you. Any place special you want to go?"

"Raah-oh-raah-raah-raah-oh-raah! Raah-oh-raah-raah!"

"Okay," I said. "The Brown Derby it is! See ya."

Bonny looked at me, aghast: "That was . . . Clyde?" I nodded and we had a wonderful lunch together. Later, we all went back to the set (Soupy's, not ours) where Bonny reunioned with Soupy and they swapped old times until it was time to roll tape. The bit being recorded had Soupy in a tux as the conductor of an unseen orchestra. He was conducting "The 1812 Overture" and, every time the playback gave off with a cannon roar, Mr. Sales was creamed with a pie from an off-camera hand, usually Clyde's. But some came from the stage manager and, at one point when there was a lull in the pastry-tossing, Clyde motioned me over, put a pie crust of shaving cream in my hand and spotted me as I hurled it—dead on-target—into the face of the star. I was instantly aware I had been awarded a rare honor.

For the next few weeks, I alternately worked on *Anson 'n' Lorrie* and poached on the set of Soupy's show. Our pilot turned out pretty good (I thought) but Mr. Silverman decided not to make it be a series. Instead, he wanted the same crew to produce a variety show starring that Jeff Altman kid (from our back-up cast) and two popular Japanese performers who were billed collectively as Pink Lady and spoke not a word of English. But that's another story for another time . . . maybe a thousand other stories for a thousand other times.

My visits to Soupy's set did not have a happy ending, either. One day, as I was slipping over to watch some of their taping and to laugh along with the crew, I arrived in time to see an ambulance pull up and its attendants break out a stretcher and hurry inside. Three minutes later, they were wheeling it out with Clyde Adler strapped to it, oxygen and intravenous fluids keeping him alive but barely. All action on the set had ceased; everyone was sitting around, pale and crying. And since I'd become a *de facto* part of the staff—and since I felt the same way they all did about him—I sat down and joined them.

Happily, Clyde Adler survived his heart attack. He gave up performing and returned to Detroit, I later heard.

Amazingly, my career survived *Pink Lady*. I did a number of other shows before ABC hired me, in 1983, to write and coproduce a special on the history of children's programming. This was one of those rare assignments were a lifetime of TV watching suddenly paid off: Everyone else involved was stunned at how much I knew without even doing a smidgen of research, not just about the shows but the names of producers, actors, and even sources for film clips. Most of the clips were located with a minimum of legwork (and a lot of haggling over fees). At one point, I spent the better part of an afternoon convincing an exec at Worldvision Syndication that they owned the rights to the *Jackson 5* cartoon show. He insisted they didn't own it, I convinced him they did . . . and he rewarded me for this information by charging us way too much for a clip.

But Soupy proved to be our biggest problem . . . especially maddening since his old show was an ABC in-house production and so were we. We contacted Soupy's agent (or manager; I forget) and got permission to include him but were told we would have to find our own film clip. Off we went in search of same, starting with the film vaults of the ABC television network.

A tired lady there informed me that, no, they had absolutely no films of *The Soupy Sales Show*. And she knew they had no films of *The Soupy Sales Show* because darn near every day, someone called up asking if they had any films of *The Soupy Sales Show* and she was getting darn sick of people calling up and asking if they had any films of *The Soupy Sales Show*. No, she told me, they had absolutely no films of *The Soupy Sales Show*, goodbye.

I hung up, discouraged. But then I got a brainstorm—or, at least, a heavy drizzle—and I phoned her back and asked if they had any films from *Lunch with Soupy Sales*. She put me on hold for about a month, then came back and said, "Oh, sure, we have tons of those." All those years, when person after person called to ask about old films, the archivist had been looking under "S" instead of "L"!

They shipped a half-dozen pristine, probably never-watched kinescopes over to us. I could probably have picked a clip from the first three minutes of any of them but, naturally, I insisted on watching all six hours. They were just as good as I remembered. We called Soupy's rep and told him about our find. And, while we were at it, we secured a phone number for Clyde Adler since he was in the clip (well, his arm was, at least). We needed his okay to include him in the show, and we'd also have to send him a check.

But the phone number turned out to be an old one with no referral . . . and a check of Detroit Information yielded no listing for "Adler,

Clyde." We spent three or four days chasing down other leads, all to no avail. The original TV White Fang, it seemed, had disappeared off the face of the earth.

All this took place in a little office at ABC, probably within fifty yards of where Soupy had originally taped his show; it was maddening that we couldn't locate Clyde Adler.

Finally, a person from the ABC Legal came by and said that, since we had no signed release from Mr. Adler, we'd have to cut him from the show and pick a new Soupy clip. "No," I said. "We are not cutting Clyde Adler out of the show. I'll find him."

I sat down at my desk and wracked my brain for another contact . . . some way to find the elusive Clyde Adler. Soupy's staff had been trying and they'd given up. I had about two hours to find him and get his okay or we'd have to cut him out of the show . . . and I was without a clue. Except . . .

On my desk—on every desk on the lot—there was a little spiral-bound ABC inter-office phone directory. All the ABC facilities around the country were linked via a central phone system. On a wild hunch, I grabbed it up and looked up the personnel of the film editing department at the ABC offices in Detroit.

There, neatly typeset, was the name "Clyde Adler" and an extension number.

I dialed the two-digit interoffice code for Detroit, then the three-digit extension given, and, so help me, the voice of White Fang answered on the other end: "Raaah-oh-raah?"

We'd spent weeks searching for Clyde Adler's phone number and it had been sitting on all our desks all along. Clyde passed away a few years ago [he died in 1993]. Soupy remains active and continues to receive all manner of well-deserved honors, not the least of which is of the one-on-one variety. When I met him and told him how much his work had meant to me. I'm sure he hears it, everywhere he goes . . . which is fine because he deserves to hear it.

But I'll bet I was one of the few to say it to Clyde Adler. I'm kinda proud of that.

• • •

WILL THE REAL SOUPY SALES PLEASE STAND UP?

Whenever someone has an encounter with a celebrity, the first question they're always asked is, "What's he (or she) really like?" People have certain perceptions of you, of course, from what they see on television. Many people, and it's understandable, think that you are who they see. I'm zany and a little crazy on TV, so that must be the way I am in real life. But it's not necessarily true. Certainly, when you're on television as much as someone like I was, it's almost impossible to hide your true personality. The camera has X ray vision—it can see through your clothing, through your psyche sometimes. You know, you can be an actor and you go on stage and you play a part, or be in a movie and people say you were very good, and you played the part well. But when you're a comedian and you're out there, you are yourself—you can't hide behind anything.

And yet, the truth is, in real life, I'm rather shy. I hate walking into a large crowd, whether it's a hotel lobby or a cocktail party or a dance. Instead, I'll head right to the nearest person I know or to the nearest bar. I'm most comfortable when I'm with people I know well. And yet I love people, I love to be around them, I love to make them laugh.

In interviews, I've sometimes been asked whether I dislike being approached in public, especially if I mind people asking for my autograph. The answer is absolutely, no. I love it, because when people don't stop me, that's when I'll start to worry. Of course, occasionally someone will stop and ask for my autograph but they think I'm someone else. In that case, I think you just have to laugh it off and try not to make that person feel embarrassed, because they usually are or would be. So, I'll just sign the other person's name. And when I'm out and I feel that people are staring at me I'm actually very flattered and happy about it. I feel as if I've accomplished something not only because I'm recognizable, but also because people think of me as a friend. And that's just the way I see myself. As a friend.

• • •

PAUL DVER:

I met Soupy when I was still in high school in Merrick, Long Island, when I was working as an intern for the sportswriter and TV commentator Dick Schaap. My father had died in 1970, when I was fifteen. My mother remarried in 1971 and we moved to Huntington, so I was kind of knocking around a lot on my own that year. Dick Schaap's mother was my French teacher, in elementary school, and when I met him and told him that my father had passed away, he took a liking to me and "hired" me as an intern at NBC.

Dick Schaap had a sports show, and he'd have a lot of celebrities and sports stars come up and do a half-hour pregame show. I met a lot of stars and for a fifteen-/sixteen-year-old kid, that was very exciting. But there were only two stars who really made a big impression on me when I met them. One was Peter Falk, who at the time had just done one season of Colombo, and the other was Soupy Sales. This was '71, so his show had only been off the air three or four years, but he was still very, very popular.

It really meant a lot to me meeting him and he was very nice to me. He asked me how I got the job and I told him that my father had died and he told me his mother had died almost at the same time, the same year, which immediately kind of gave us an instant bond. At the end of the program, I went up to him and asked, "Can I call you?"

He said, "Yeah," and then he actually gave me his phone number.

Over a period of several months, occasionally I'd call him and just say, "Hey, how you doing?" and he was always very nice to me.

I'd tell my friends, "I'm friends with Soupy Sales." And of course they'd say to me, "You're full of shit."

The reason I was interested in working at NBC is because I wanted to be an actor. I had been acting in New York, studying with Stella Adler on Saturdays, and I was taking it pretty seriously for a kid from Long Island. At this particular time I was appearing in a play in Huntington, with a friend of mine. We were doing a double feature. It was a Howard Pinter play, The Dumb Waiter, and the second half was a multimedia play done by the PA multimedia. They wanted to do something that went from stage to film, and they knew I was kind of a half-ass actor and they asked, "Would you direct this?"

Me and the Turtles, Flo and Eddie, in the 1970s.

With Alice Cooper, Los Angeles show.

I said, "Okay, but how are we going to fill up this auditorium?" It wasn't like it was a class play with all the kids in it. It was just me and this other guy. So I thought about it for a while and then I said, "Well, let's call Soupy."

So I called Soupy and I said, "If I brought you a tape recorder would you do a commercial for our production and then I could run it on the school public address system and maybe even put it on WGSM radio?" I had already called up WGSM radio station, and asked, "Would you play a commercial for our play if Soupy Sales does the read?" And they said "Yes."

Surprisingly, Soupy said, "Okay, meet me at the set of *What's My Line?*" I went backstage at *What's My Line?*—which was exciting in itself, because I loved watching him on that show, and there I was backstage with Arlene Francis and Larry Blyden, Jack Cassidy, and Soupy.

After the show, I showed Soupy the script I'd written for the commercial and he read it into my tape recorder and did some improv-ing around it. It turned out to be very funny.

We played the commercial on the radio and the school intercom, and I remember kids came up to me at school and asked, "Is that Soupy Sales?"

So, here I am, a sixteen-year-old kid and Soupy Sales was doing favors for me. I couldn't believe it!

I made it a point to keep up with Soup and, after a while, he said to me, "Paul, why don't you come on down to watch me on *What's My Line?*" And so almost every time he did *What's My Line*, I'd go and hang out with him at the show.

I guess the basis of our friendship was that I was a kid who loved him and had an interest in the business and I have to say that he was and always has been very responsive to his fans. And, as I said, I think there was also a little bit of a bond between us that had to do with the fact that we each just lost a parent. Maybe it was like both of us felt a little lost about it. And because we looked at each other that way, we got close.

One day he called to tell me that he was going to play a club and asked me, "Do you want to come and see my act?"

"Hey, I'd love to," I said.

I remember I took a gang of friends with me and we laughed our asses off. I mean, he was amazing in a club. I had no idea that he could be that funny. He was just amazing and funny.

It was just him telling jokes, with jokes that led into other jokes within jokes, old jokes, new jokes, jokes I hadn't heard, everything had been strung together so fast, and coming out so energetic from such a funny delivery. He captivated everybody. He also had a band and he did some musical bits. Then, at the end of the act, he did a salute to his old show.

After the show ended, I went back stage and said, "Wow, thanks for inviting me." And then I said, "If you ever need a piano player, I'm available."

So he said, "Oh, okay, yeah, one day you'll do that for me."

I never thought he actually would but, as it turned out, he was true to his word. And he really cares about other people.

People often ask me, "What's Soupy really like?" Well, here's a story that tells it like he is.

Soupy was flying somewhere on an airline when they used to serve steak for dinner. So, Soupy ordered steak and they brought it over and he starts to eat and he sees a guy in front of him and he's got steak sauce. So, Soupy calls the stewardess over and says, "Excuse me, but can I have a little steak sauce for my steak?"

She says, "We don't have any steak sauce."

Soupy says, "Well, the guy over there has steak sauce."

She says, "Well, I don't know how he got that steak sauce, but we don't serve steak sauce."

Soupy says, "Well, you should serve steak sauce on the flight. You're serving steak, so why not serve steak sauce?"

She says, "Well, why don't you write a letter to the airline and Frank Borman," the former astronaut, who was president of the airline at that time, "and tell him that you want steak sauce to be served on the flight."

So, Soupy decides he's going to sit down and write a letter to Frank Borman. He writes something like, "Dear Frank, you're serving steak on your planes, I think you should serve a little steak sauce." So, he sends the letter and he forgets about it.

One day, back in New York, Soupy calls me up, all excited, and he says, "Paul, I got a letter from Frank Borman." He said, "Mr. Sales, we received your letter, and you're right. We should serve steak sauce with our steaks. We gave your suggestion to the chef and we're going to take care of that right away."

Soupy thought, "I did something good."

About two weeks later, Soupy comes home, and there's a crate outside of his door, He opens it up and there's about a million little packets of steak sauce. And Soupy says to himself, "What am I gonna do with all this steak sauce?" So, he tried to give some to me, "You want some steak sauce, Paul?" and when I hesitated he said, "Well, Paul, you might as well take some now, because you never know." Finally, he threw out a bunch of those little packets, but he kept some and when he'd fly, he'd put a couple of those packets in his pocket.

A year or so later, he's flying out of town again and, of course, he's got his steak sauce with him. He orders a steak and when it comes he takes the little packet out of his pocket, tears it open and puts it on his steak. After he does this, a guy sitting behind him rings the stewardess, who comes over and says, "What's the problem, sir?"

The guy says, "I'd like some steak sauce."

"We don't serve steak sauce," the stewardess says.

"Well, why does he get it?" he asks, gesturing toward Soupy. "Is he a special privileged character?"

Well, Soupy hears this and turns around and gives the guy steak sauce. And the next thing he knew he was handing steak sauce out all over the plane. That was Soupy . . .

Sha-Na-Na—*I guess I pissed them off, but I have no idea what I could have said.*

WNBC Radio, 1984.

9

Radio Daze

New York, 1985–1988

Nut-at-the-Door: Mr. Sales. Mr. Sales. You've gotta help me.
Soupy: What's wrong?
Nut-at-the-Door: It's my wife. She thinks she's a pretzel.
Soupy: So why don't you take her to a psychiatrist?
Nut-at-the-Door: I did. He says she's twisted.

· · ·

In 1985 an opportunity to return to radio came my way and I grabbed it. I was excited to get back into a medium where my roots were—those days on the air on my college station, WHTN, were some of the happiest times of my life. I remember a reporter once asked me if it was a step down for me to go back into radio, and I replied, "No. Frank Sinatra doesn't play New York all the time." Besides, I didn't see it that way. Radio has always fascinated me, the possibilities of radio have always intrigued me. It is, as I've said before, theater of the mind, and there were so many creative things I could do with it. In many ways it allowed me to do so much more and be so much more than I was on television.

By 1984, the nightclub gigs I'd been doing regularly were slowing down and John Hayes at NBC was looking to put somebody on the radio between Howard Stern and Don Imus. One night, he happened to see me perform at the Bottom Line and I guess he said to himself, "Gee, I'd like to put Soupy on the air and then I'd have the greatest lineup in radio." And that's just what he did.

And so, with an offer from WNBC radio to go on between Howard Stern and Don Imus—a perfect spot for me, I thought—I went about gathering a talented bunch of folks that included Ray D'ariano, Paul Dver, and Judy D'Angelis who did the news.

Ray D'ariaNo:

After I coproduced his album, *Still Soupy After All These Years*, Soupy and I remained friends. We used to have lunch together at the Friars Club, and once he showed me a humorous unpublished novel that he had written about a cab driver who was also a werewolf.

During this period, I had an idea for a movie, and one day I told Soupy about it and he was very encouraging. He even started casting the movie. The idea was to make a movie about a wedding band, who were now middle-aged guys who all had other jobs and did this in their spare time. But they'd been a band since high school. And on the weekends, despite their problems, they'd still get together and do gigs, and that's when they're really the most alive.

Soupy loved it. In his head, he cast Steve Lawrence as the singer, and Walter Matthau and Tony Randall, who was going to be the drummer, would also be in the group. Every time I saw him after that, he'd say, "Well how's the script going? I've got a great idea—you know in the wedding when the kids slide on the thing and blah, blah, blah." He had me continually laughing.

Finally, one day I said to him, "Soupy, do you want to write this script with me?"

He said, "Sure," so I wrote the treatment and got it to Mel and Diane Sokolow at Warner Brothers. They liked it and asked for a meeting with me and Soupy and the result was that we got a movie deal with Warner Brothers.

During the writing of the script, which was called *The Wedding Band*,

Soupy would contribute his funny ideas and jokes. And all during that time I couldn't believe that I was writing a script with *Soupy Sales*.

The movie never got made, but if you know anything about the film business that isn't that unusual.

I then got a job writing for Jay Thomas, for his radio show on WKTU, which eventually evolved into me performing characters with Jay on his show.

One day Soupy calls me up and tells me he's been hired to do a radio show on WNBC and that he would like me to come on and do what I do on Jay's show. "I'm going to be sandwiched between Imus and Howard Stern," he said, and I thought, "Wow, that's pretty good."

Imus was on first and then we were on the air from 10 A.M. till 3 P.M. and then Howard came on. Although I don't think the public realized it, each one of those shows had the exact same format. They had the guy, the co-host, comedy writer, characters, producer, etc. It really was the same format from 5:30 in the morning until 7:30 at night. Essentially, what we had was three variations on the same theme.

Howard Stern loved Soupy, and I remember his first day on the air, Howard came in and gave him a gift of a book of Bob and Ray radio routines. Soupy appreciated the gesture very much.

The concept of the show included band music similar to that used on *The Tonight Show*, and sound effects like applause. It was going to be kind of like Theatre of the Mind, kind of like *The Tonight Show*, but on the radio. The picture listeners were supposed to get was of Soupy on the couch with his sidekick, me, and the orchestra was over there, and the audience was over here, kind of thing. I think it worked pretty well for the average listener.

We would get to the studio at 8:30, so we could write stuff for the show. It was pretty much of a regular format and Soupy was thriving on it. It was the greatest thing in the world for him, because all of the sudden, he was back in the spotlight. Perhaps he wasn't nationwide, but he was in the number one market in the country with two of the wildest radio guys ever. He was back.

The two prime spots, as you know, are the morning and evening drive times. Our show was just the link to hold them together: Soupy Sales between Imus and Howard—and WNBC milked the hell out of it. They had posters with Imus and Howard wearing devil horns and with

Soupy between them. Our show lasted two and a half years.

As far as the show was concerned, Soupy came out and did his monologue, which might consist of some comedy bits or him commenting about current events.

After we chatted about the events of the day, there was music played, whatever NBC was playing at the time, the Top 40, for instance, and then there were call-ins. We'd get calls from Soupy's fans, telling him how much they loved him, and Soupy was always very, very, very, very nice to his fans, both on the air and in person. Then Soupy would chat with the bandleader, who was played by me.

At lunchtime the show was supposed to be coming from the NBC Commissary and we had all the appropriate sound effects of the restaurant. This was the segment of the show that would feature the day's interviews, where guests would come and have lunch with Soupy in a booth in the cafeteria, just like in Sardi's. We had people like Cab Calloway, Dizzy Gillespie, and a lot of other jazz people. And sometimes we had the wrestlers on, people like Rowdy Roddy Piper and Bobby "the Brain" Heenan, or whoever else was big at the time. The wrestlers were always fun because they really got into it. And then we also had celebrities like Renee Taylor and Joe Bologna, Linda Lavin, or anyone else who might be promoting something.

James Brown in particular stands out as a guest. That was quite a day. James had a book out and the thought of Soupy and James Brown talking together really had me pumped up. I thought, "This is going to be great!"

Anyway, James Brown shows up and it's like he's on another planet. He was just flying so high on something. They bring him in the studio, and he just did not know where he was. Soupy would say something like, "James, how you doing?"

And Brown was like a zombie, and he was saying things like, "Why am I here?"

I held up his book and I said, "To promote your book."

And he'd say, "What book?"

When we heard this we said to ourselves, "Uh-oh." So, he never actually made it onto the air.

We also had characters like the French maitre d', played by Soupy's piano player from his live act, Paul Dver, who would say things like,

"Monsieur Soupy, how are you today?" kind of a take-off of Curly from *The Three Stooges*. Speaking of Paul, to me, this was one of the most generous things Soupy ever did, because everything on the show, including a full orchestra, was on tape. But Soupy had them put a piano in the studio just so Paul could come in and play it.

· · ·

My idea was to do a show that would be kind of a variety talk show. I'd do a monologue. I'd play music. I'd do interviews. I'd take phone calls. We'd do the news, weather and traffic report, of course. And I'd have a stable of funny characters, played by Ray and Paul, that would appear regularly on the show. It was kind of a throwback to the earlier days of radio and, once again, it gave me a wonderful opportunity to create a theater of the mind.

PAUL DVER:

I was a regular on the show, appearing every day. I had been on the radio with Mark Simone. Mark Simone was on WMCA, and I was "Mr. Keys." And I would play for auditions and *Name That Tune*. And it was mostly comedy, because we'd put down the callers, having fun with phone callers, and when Soupy got the call, I went, "Well, I've done a lot of radio."

Soupy said, "Well, we'll see what happens."

The fact is, I almost didn't get hired at all. But Soupy fought for me. He said he wanted a piano in the studio, and he wanted me to come on with him and play the piano or maybe do some of the stuff I did with Mark Simone. Soupy argued for me, saying, "Paul's good. It'll work out." Soupy really went to bat for me, which I really needed at the time, because the club work had slowed down and I was wondering what I'd do.

They put the piano in the studio and they brought me in. But they decided that they couldn't pay me to do full time. So I came in and did two hours—essentially from twelve to two o'clock. From twelve to one, I was a character at the cafeteria, because that's when they had had Soupy eating lunch at the fake commissary. I came in as Jerry the Waiter. I'd have to write this routine every night and give it to Soupy before we did it at noon. We'd read it through together and the I would do Curly, from the *Three Stooges*, as the waiter, because Curly's real name was Jerry. So I said, "I'll be Jerry the Waiter. Eh, cointenlee." Every day and I'd show Soupy what I'd written and I'd say, "Okay, let's read it through." Or I'd just read it to him. And that's all he'd need. He'd do straight from me.

And after the first couple of times, I learned the formula that he wanted, and the formula that worked best. It was tough for me, I couldn't go to sleep if I didn't have the page, even if it was one in the morning. I wouldn't dare fall asleep because I'd wake up and go, "Where's the page?" So I had to make sure, not only that it was written, but that it was funny. It was done exactly as written. Soupy and I had no time to change it. If something went wrong, we would ad-lib through it.

I did that from twelve to one, which was great, because I was also interacting with the guest stars because that's when he did the star interview. Then, from one to two, I'd come in as his pianist. He'd introduce me. And during that hour, I was myself. And then maybe we'd do some kind of game, maybe we'd do a new audition, once in a while or something like that.

Ray was doing a lot of characters, too. He was doing Daryl Morticom, who was the bandleader of the show. NBC had these tracks, and they wanted it to sound like kind of a talk show where a band plays in and out of commercials. So they needed someone to say they were in the band. And Ray did a black man, which Soupy liked a lot.

After a while I got a call. "NBC really likes you. They want to give you a raise. And they want you to come in as kind of a producer also," which was fine with me.

Then they added, "We're gonna be doing network show with Soupy called *Moldy Oldies*, and we want you to do Jerry and we also want you to do Marvin the Barber," which was another character that I developed after about four or five months. We didn't do that show live. We would tape that in the studio on Thursday; we'd have to tape four or five in a row. And then they spread them out during the week and played them. That went on for two years.

The first thing I remember is people's reaction to me sitting there as this cool guy and then I'd say, "Ok, now I'm going to do a character who serves us the waiter." And to see the reaction, the transition on their faces, because I was doing this insane idiot. And, some people who were very creative themselves, Steve Allen or somebody like that, would understand completely, but you're sitting there with some people and they wouldn't know what the hell I was doing. I remember one time Robert Vaughan who used to play Napoleon Solo in *The Man From U.N.C.L.E.* was a guest and I was doing Jerry, saying something like, "Afterwards Napoleon and I are gonna go out and get some chicks."

And he went, "No, don't say that!" He was taking it so seriously that it really cracked me up.

James Brown, "The Hardest Working Man In Show Business," came on one time, and I don't know what he was on. He had a lot of guys with him, they looked armed. This was before he went to prison. He sat down and we got ready to go and he turned to me and he said, "Where the fuck am I?"

I said, "You're at NBC."

He said, "What the fuck am I doing here?"

I said, "I think we're going to interview you. You're gonna go on the radio with Soupy. You know Soupy."

And he looked around, he was all paranoid, and he said again, "Where the fuck am I?"

This went on for about five minutes. And you know, he's getting like crazy, like, "What the fuck? Where am I?"

I said, "Soupy, something's wrong with him."

Soupy said, "I'm not putting him on the air." And, remember, he had just promoted for two days, "James Brown's gonna be on, the King of Soul is going to be on our show." So, Soupy went over to James Brown's people and he said, "We're not gonna let him come on. Take him home." And they did. They just pulled him right out of the studio. So he never went on the air that day. But Soupy was very professional about it. He never said anything on the air. We did a couple of James Brown jokes. But we didn't really explain that he was there and in trouble.

One day Cab Calloway, one of Soupy's favorites, was on the air and Soupy said, "Hey Cab, how you doing? You working the Cotton Club? Blah, blah, blah." Calloway had these keys in his hand, and he kept bouncing his keys on the board, and in the studio you never do that, because it echoes all through the place. So, he was bouncing his keys and looking at Soupy and he'd answer in one word answers. "So

The gang from the NBC radio show, 1985. From left: Bruce Leonard, the engineer; Paul Dver; Judy D'Angelis, who did the news; me; Ray D'ariano; and the producer, Rodney Belizaire.

you've worked with this, you've work with that. How was Duke Ellington at the Cotton Club?"

And he'd bounce the keys and go, "Yep."

Soupy would say, "Well, when you started out did you have a hard time . . . ?"

Calloway would say, "Nope."

So Soupy just danced live on the air like that for about ten minutes, and finally he went to a commercial—I remember Stan Scotland had brought Cab Calloway over—and Stan Scotland said, "When we come back, ask Cab about the races, he loves the races."

And Soupy shook his head and said, "When we come back, he's gone."

There's a funny story about Robin Williams. Robin and I knew each other from the old days, and at this point in time, it must have been around 1986, Robin was hosting *Saturday Night Live*. So, Ray and Soupy said, "Robin Williams is around. He was a friend of yours, Paul, wasn't he? Why don't you get him and bring him down?"

I didn't have much choice, so I went upstairs, to studio 8-H, where they taped *Saturday Night Live*. I got off the elevator on the eighth floor and I look down the long hall and I see Robin, just standing there alone. Robin and I used to be close, I mean very close, back in the days when we were both getting started.

Anyway, Robin's all the way down the hall and I see him. I hadn't seen him since he'd starred in the movie, *Popeye*, when we'd had a reunion at Chumley's. So, I'm coming down the hall and I'm getting closer to him and I go, "Hey." And I expected that I'd get a "Hey," back from him.

"So listen," I said, "they asked me to come up here and ask you if you want to come down to the studio to meet Soupy. Do you want to come down?"

"Well, I'm rehearsing," he said.

"We're on the second floor, just come on down." And I gave him the hours we'd be there. "We'd be thrilled to have you on, Robin, but if you can't, you can't." He was acting as if he wasn't going to do it, so I shrugged and said, "No problem. Good seeing you, Robin. Hey, man, you're doing so great."

"Robin, don't worry about it man," I said. "Everything's cool."

In the meantime, Whoopi saw all this going on and she asked Robin, "Who is this?"

"Oh, it's an old friend of mine from Juilliard."

Anyway, they said, "Well, we're going to get ready to go on Joey Reynolds."

I said, "Do you want to meet Soupy, do you want to say hi to Soupy?"

Robin says, "Yeah. I don't know if I have time." He says, "Tell Soupy to come on over, I'd love to say hello."

Well, this went back and forth for a while, until I was finally able to bring them together outside Soupy's office.

Robin said, "Oh, hello Mr. S."

Soupy says, "Hey Robin, nice to meet you. You know, you're really talented."

"Oh, I grew up watching you. I'm a big fan of yours. Blah, blah, blah."

That was the only time Soupy and Robin met. And that was thanks to my diligent work, but as you can see, it wasn't easy.

There's another story that comes to mind about Soupy and Buddy Rich, the drummer. Buddy loved comedians, and he loved Soupy who, as it happened, was something of a drummer himself. A lot of people in the business were close to Buddy, people like Mel Torme, Mel Brooks—they all grew up in the same Brooklyn neighborhood as Buddy did. Soupy introduced Buddy and I a couple of times, and Buddy was very nice to me. It's funny, when I meet musicians, they always say, "Oh, Buddy's a prick." And I say, to me, he's always been like Uncle Buddy—he smiles, he hugs me.

Anyway, at this particular time, Soupy and I were in Chicago, or Detroit, I don't remember where, and quite often stars would stop by and see us if they were in town. I was in my room watching the basketball playoff game—it was the Lakers against somebody and they were playing in Los Angeles. Soupy called my room and he said, "Guess who's coming to see us tonight?"

"Who?" I said.

"Buddy Rich."

"Really, I don't think he's ever seen us perform," I said.

"He hasn't," said Soupy. But he said he's gonna come by tonight and he said he wanted guest passes for four."

Me and Billy Joel, doing my WNBC radio show, 1987.

"So, give it to him," I said.

"Oh, I will. In fact, he said, he might come downstairs in the hotel and we can have a drink together."

"That's cool," I said,

"So, I'm going to go down and have a drink with him."

So I hung up the phone and I continued watching the game, and all of a sudden they say on the TV, "And look who's sitting on the court tonight, we have a few celebrities." And they show a picture of Tony Danza sitting there and there's Jack Nicholson, who's always at the Laker games. And then, look who's there—Buddy Rich. And remember, they're playing in Los Angeles. Live.

So, I pick up the phone and I call Soupy's room. When he picks up the phone, I ask, "Who told you they're coming to see you in Detroit tonight?"

"Buddy Rich."

"Exactly what did he say?"

"He said he's here and he wants to come see the show tonight. He wants tickets for four."

What else did he say?"

"He said, 'Well, you might not recognize me because I won't be wearing my toupeé.'"

"Soupy," I said, "turn on Channel 4."

"Why?"

"Turn on Channel 4, just watch for a minute."

So, Soupy turns on the TV and he's watching and after a few minutes the camera pans the fans again and I said to Soupy, "Soupy, take a look at that. Buddy Rich is sitting there. He's in Los Angeles. So, who the hell called you?"

"Really?"

"Yeah, really. Buddy Rich is in Los Angeles. Some guy who probably thinks he looks like Buddy Rich is trying to take you for a ride."

So sure enough the guy calls Soupy back and says, "Hey Soupy, I'm downstairs, you want to have that drink?"

And Soupy says, "You're not Buddy Rich. My conductor Paul just saw Buddy Rich in Los Angeles at the basketball game."

And he says, "No."

Later, I said to Soupy, "Soupy, you should have known, why would he say to you 'You won't recognize me, I'm not wearing my toupee.' Why would Buddy Rich ever say that to anybody on the phone?"

And Soupy goes, "Oh, it's some schmuck." Later, we told Buddy that story and he loved it.

JOYCE KELLER, PSYCHIC COUNSELOR and GUEST ON SOUPY'S NBC RADIO SHOW

The first time I heard Soupy's name was when my young children, Elaine and Scott, were watching television, and screaming with laughter. When I asked them what they were watching, and what was so funny, Elaine said, "Soupy Sales! He's throwing pies and talking like a dog!"

"That doesn't sound great," I said, "why don't you watch something educational?" They both looked at me, and gave me a look that said that I just didn't get it!

So I sat down with them and watched Soupy Sales for the first time. They were right. He was very funny. I found myself laughing in spite of myself.

A short time later, I found out that many children, probably including mine, had caused Soupy to be suspended from his TV show. It was in response to Soupy's New Year's Day morning joke about how children should go "quietly into your sleeping parents' bedroom, into your daddy's wallet, and to send the money to Soupy at Channel 5." In gratitude, he would send the children a "postcard from Puerto Rico." Soupy was suspended shortly after that.

By the mid-'80s, I was a tried-and-true Soupy fan. I was delighted that Soupy was on NBC radio, and that I could hear him and laugh with him five days a week. My joy increased, however, when I was invited to come on the air with Soupy once or twice a week, so that I could do psychic readings for his listeners.

Being on NBC with Soupy wasn't always easy, but it was always fun. It really was a "party on the air." Soupy and his crew threw paper planes and joked about everything and everyone. But in true, classy, Soupy Sales style, he was never off-color or offensive. I found that amazing. He never offended anyone, and was always so gracious to his crew, listeners, and guests. Soupy always thanked his on-air guests

The horse named after me—it actually won a purse of $13,000
and I didn't get a penny. Not even any oats.

when their visit was finished, and again at the close of his show. He never failed to plug books, plays, shows, appearances, and anything else that was important to his guests.

Sometimes, though, it was challenging when a call came in from a listener who had a serious problem. The air-time was short, the pressure was great, and Soupy wanted, of course, to maintain an air of lightness and humor. Frequently, though, my problem was that a listener needed more than a "quick fix." For example, one day a young man named Gary called in, and asked a question about his health. As Soupy sent a paper plane sailing through my hair, Gary said, "Joyce, I'm having a test tomorrow . . . I've been diagnosed with a serious blood disease. My doctor tells me that I may have only a short time to live."

I swallowed hard, and felt inspired to say to him, "Gary, you're going to be amazed and happy with the results of the test. I feel that you're going to be celebrating when you get the results, and that you're going to be fine!"

I was thinking to myself that I probably shouldn't show up for the next show, because Gary's relatives would be calling in to tell me off, or have me thrown out of NBC. Instead, the following week, Gary called in again. He was jubilant. "Joyce, you were 100 percent right . . . the tests all came back negative. The doctors are amazed. I'm going to celebrate!" Soupy looked at me, and gave me a big smile and a thumbs-up sign. I can't tell you what a special moment in my life that was. Soupy's approval added enormously to this very special radio moment.

During another appearance on his show, I said to Soupy, "Soupy, your wife has to watch her bag this weekend. Have her grip it tightly when you go out." The following week, Soupy told on the air a story about how his wife Trudy had lost her handbag, and it was found in a tree!

Soupy never hesitated to confirm correct predictions on the air. He was always so gracious. If I made a mistake, he glossed over it, and never mentioned it.

I've been on many radio and television shows, but I have never received more considerate treatment from any broadcast host than from Soupy. The first time I was on NBC, Soupy personally escorted me to the Payroll Department, and said, "Please put this woman on the payroll!" Those were magic words. They were words that helped me many times over the years. Not only with the payment itself, but also with the medical and other benefits. What a considerate gentleman.

Another time, when the radio show was over, Soupy offered to have his limo drop me off at Penn Station. Since it was very cold out, and he always made me laugh, I was delighted to accept his offer. It turned out that it wasn't that simple. Even though it was just a short walk from the studio, to the elevator, out through the RCA building to the limo, it was an interminable period of time. Soupy graciously stopped every two feet, so that he could sign autographs and speak with fans. I think that what was normally a five-minute walk took closer to an hour. Even though it was freezing out, Soupy stood on the sidewalk for over half an hour shaking hands with fans, and telling them jokes. It was an amazing sight. I felt very privileged to call him my friend. Eventually, we got in the limo, and he dropped me off at Penn Station. It was really an inspiring experience.

My husband Jack and I have also seen Soupy perform live comedy shows in Atlantic City, Connecticut, and New York. We were always invited to his dressing room after the show. It always amazed me that he had made something so difficult look so easy. The proof that it had been hard work was that he always had a big towel around his neck, and he was saturated with perspiration. He always deserved every penny of what he earned.

Soupy and his wife, Trudy, are truly gracious. These wonderful people never forget our birthdays and holidays. Soupy and Trudy have often left singing birthday messages on our answering machine.

· · ·

Eventually, WNBC decided to tinker with our show—do you see a pattern here?—and I wouldn't have it. Like everything else, radio was changing. The shock jocks, like Howard Stern and Don Imus, were taking over, and I guess there was no room for shows like mine. I was disappointed, of course, but as I've said before, sometimes being fired or canceled shakes you out of your complacency. I think we were doing a good show and I think people liked what we were doing, but the station didn't think so and when they wanted me to do something I wasn't comfortable with, I just decided to take a walk. It wasn't that I necessarily had someplace else to go, it's just that I had faith that something else would turn up and, even if it didn't, after all these years I wasn't about to be in a situation where I wasn't happy and where I wasn't being appreciated.

And so I left radio and, in a manner of speaking, went back on the road again.

10

WHAT DO YOU MEAN BY THAT?

NEW YORK, 1990 to tHe PRESENT

AL ROKER, AT SOUPY'S 75TH BiRTHDAY AT THE FRiAR'S CLUB

I was a young kid, and the first time I saw Soupy Sales, he looked at me and said, "Shine 'em up, kid." I was a kid who was just enthralled by Soupy and I wanted to be just like him. And, at twelve years old, I had the black sweater and the red-and-white polka-dot bow tie, the chinos, and I used to get the crap kicked out of me in my neighborhood. You know people would say, "What the hell is your problem, boy? I'll kick your ass." And that was my dad! And "Hey, do the Mouse." Who knew that this in Italian had something to do with a donkey, your mother and . . .

But I really was influenced by Soupy. True story—in 1964, I came in second place to four white girls lip-synching "I Want to Hold Your Hand" in the New York City Parks Department Talent Contest. I did the

Mouse with a ventriloquist dummy. And that was my introduction to show business. And it's been downhill ever since.

I was talking to Soupy this evening upstairs and he told me that ever since he and Trudy got into S & M, the sex has been great. And I said, "Soupy, I don't want to know about this."

And he said, 'No, really, you might want to think about it.'

And I said, "Why?"

And he said, "Well, it's the S & M. Trudy sleeps and I masturbate."

. . .

You won't see me much on television anymore—the business has undergone tremendous changes since I began in Cincinnati half a century ago—but that doesn't mean that I'm not alive and kicking . . . and working. Now, I'm a movie star . . . okay, not exactly a star in the sense that Tom Cruise and Brad Pitt are, though given the opportunity I'm sure I could give them a run for their money, which I wish I had, by the way.

In 1994, I appeared in *And God Spoke*, which is about two guys who get fifteen million dollars to make a Bible movie and they blow their money in the first week. So, in the second week, instead of being able to afford the money to get Charlton Heston to play Moses, they get yours truly, Soupy Sales. Type-casting, if you ask me. By now, it's become kind of a cult favorite. As a matter of fact, as I was channel surfing the other night, I caught the last half hour of it on some cable channel, so I'm sure somewhere, there's an audience for it. I remember my last line, as the credits role, they had actors in the film and others give testimonials. Mine was, "If this isn't the best movie I've ever seen, let me be struck dumb." That's where my acting ability was really tested. Overall, the critics were rather kind to me. "Sales' moments on screen have got to be among the funniest of the year," was how the *Los Angeles Times* put it.

Besides spending my time starring (okay, appearing) in movies, I still perform my nightclub act, taking it on the road as much as possible (after all, a moving target is harder to hit). Let's face it, I'd work the back of a cab, so long as I got paid. I don't get hit by pies unless I get paid, but if you got hit with a pie, you'd want some money with it, wouldn't you?

I especially like to go back to Detroit, where I have so many fans, and, of course, down to Huntington where I love performing for my hometown pals. Lately, they've put together period reunions, which are terrific fun for me, swapping stories about old times.

CHaRLiE Cook:

Whenever Soupy comes to town we party like crazy. Well, one time he came down and we'd been partying for two or three nights and I got home at four o'clock in the morning. I had a drug store and I usually opened up at nine o'clock in the morning, but I was just too tired to get out of bed. Well, the phone rings a little after nine and it was Soupy.

"What are you doing?" he asks.

"I'm getting ready to go to work," I say. "Where are you?"

"I'm inside your drugstore," he says, "waiting for you."

He'd actually gotten there early in the morning and convinced one of the employees to let him in.

When Soupy comes down here he often performs. I remember he was here in Huntington doing a series of shows at the Holiday back in the 1970s and we all went out to see him perform. My wife and I were sitting there and the band started to play some real good music, so I said to my wife, "Grace, let's dance." It turned out that it was Soupy's introduction music and I guess if we'd had a little less to drink, we'd have known it. Finally, a friend of mine came over to us and said, "Come on, Charlie, sit down, this is Soupy's introduction." Soupy was standing in the wings, waiting to come on, and someone came over to him and said, "There are a couple of nuts out there, dancing." Soupy looks out and says, "Hell, that's not a nut, that's my best friend, Charlie Cook." Then, when he came onstage to do his act, he pointed to me and said, "That's my best friend, Charlie Cook, and he not only sells drugs"— referring to the fact that I'm a pharmacist—"he takes 'em, too."

• • •

I had an unfortunate accident in 1995 that slowed me somewhat. I was hosting the Daytime Emmy Awards in New York City and I walked backstage where they had no lights or railing. I fell and tore my quadriceps tendon that controls my leg, and it never quite healed correctly, making it a little difficult for me to get around. But although I'm seventy-five now, I take good care of myself. Every morning I get up, I feel like a twenty-year-old. Unfortunately, there's never one around.

PAUL DVER:

Even after the club dates dried up, Soupy and I stayed close. One day, in 1995, Soup was tabbed to do the local Emmy Awards, at the Copacabana, in New York, on 57th Street. He said to me, "Why don't you come over and watch me emcee and then we can have dinner?"

So I went over, and they started taping, but there was a technical problem—they had to restart the whole thing because of the cameras and the sound. So it had been like an hour and a half, and they were going to go back and start at the beginning. And I said, "Soupy, I can't stick around."

He said, "I'll tell you what—go home for like the two hours and then come back when dinner's served."

So I went home and the phone rang and it was Trudy and she told me that Soupy was in the hospital. "He fell off the back stage, couldn't see the steps," she told me.

Since then, I've had friends tell me—they've done shows at the Copa—you can't see the steps there—you see the lights, it looks like it's coming down, but the steps are over there. So a lot of people have told me they know how Soupy fell. And I don't know what happened when he fell, but it was a bad fall and it started a chain reaction off. He's had continuous surgery and—it was just hard for him to walk at first.

But now he's back on his feet again, and we're doing shows again, taking clips of his old shows, talking about them, taking questions from the audience. Everyone seems to like what we do and they especially enjoy seeing Soupy on the stage again.

· · ·

Over the years, I've certainly had my share of awards and honors. I may not be in the Baseball Hall of Fame, but I am in the Hall of Fame of both Huntington High School and the city of Huntington.

Trudy and me at WXYZ Tribute in Detroit, 1998.

My "cast" today

Me and Tony

Me and Hunt

Me, Kevin Butler, and Frank Nastasi

Charlie Cook and Bill Cravens

Me and Dave Usher

In 1990, I received a special Emmy Award from the Detroit chapter of the Capital Television Academy for contributions to television. In addition, I've been inducted into the Museum of Broadcasting and received the Television Academy Silver Circle Award for twenty-five years in the industry.

But perhaps the most touching and wonderful moment for me came when the Friars Club threw a special celebration last year for my seventy-fifth birthday, January 8, 2001. I was so grateful for those who came to honor me, especially those who gave of their time and talent to perform, people like emcee Mickey Freeman (who made quite a name for himself appearing on Phil Silvers's classic *Sergeant Bilko*); comedians Larry Storch, Jeffrey Ross, Perry Gardner, Andrea Roman, Uncle Floyd Vivino, Susie Essman, Prof. Irwin Corey, and Pat Cooper; singers Jackie Paris, Beverly "Goldie" Dver, Annie Ross, Marlene Verplanck; and, of course, the inimitable weatherman and bon vivant, Al Roker.

But for me, perhaps the most touching moment came when a letter from my son Tony, who unfortunately couldn't be there that night, was read to me and the audience. Here's what he wrote:

"I'm so proud to have a father that has meant the world to others. A father that was a hero to so many children. This is a letter I found on the Internet that is one small example of the way that you touched people's lives. Now, here's the letter. 'When I was a little girl in Detroit, during the '50s, I was very lonely. My father was an alcoholic, my mother took prescription drugs. They were so involved with their own problems. I was alone most of the time. I would run home for lunch every day to eat with Soupy Sales. It was like having lunch every day with a friend. I never met him, but I want to thank him for all those lunches that I didn't have to eat alone. Sincerely, Janet Daines.' Happy birthday, Dad, I love you, Tony."

It was difficult to follow that, but trouper than I am, I did.

"I usually don't go on this early," I said. "But this is a wonderful night. I can't tell you how much I appreciate you guys coming out. It really is something. I can't thank you enough. I do want to tell you that the great thing about turning seventy-five is, you don't get any more calls from insurance salesmen. I do want to thank Mickey Freeman and I also want to pay tribute to my beautiful wife, Trudy. And thank you so very much for coming out." A little choked with emotion, I added, "I'm having a little trouble with my voice, I swallowed a shot glass a while ago. But, I thank you so very much and until I see you again, I love you very much. Thank you very much for a great evening."

And a great evening it was. And I hope that at my one hundredth birthday bash it's even better.

SOUPYOGRAPHY!
SOUPY'S TELEVISION
APPEARANCES FROM 1955-1999

SOUPY SALES!
ABC, WEEKNIGHTS: MONDAY, JULY 4, 1955–FRIDAY, AUGUST 26, 1955.
Head Puppeteer/Comedy Asistant: Clyde Adler
Theme song composed and arranged by Bill Snyder

Set against the backdrop of the living room of his house, Soupy Sales performs comedy skits, jokes, puns, songs, and dance numbers while trying to supress the antics of his puppet pals.

LUNCH WITH SOUPY SALES!
ABC, SATURDAY AFTERNOONS: OCTOBER 3, 1959–MARCH 25, 1961
Head Puppeteer/Comedy Assistant: Clyde Adler
Theme song composed and arranged by Bill Snyder
"The Soupy Shuffle" composed and arranged by Mortimer, performed by Soupy Sales

Soupy performs jokes, puns, comedy skits, and song and dance numbers while eating lunch with his viewers and his puppet friends. Based on a TV comedy series that Sales and Adler hosted on weekday afternoons on WXYZ-TV, Channel 7 in Detroit. The duo also hosted a weekday morning version of this series: *Breakfast with Soupy Sales!* also in Detroit.

THE SOUPY SALES SHOW!
ABC, FRIDAY EVENINGS: JANUARY 26, 1962–APRIL 13, 1962
Head Puppeteer/Comedy Asistant: Clyde Adler

As a Friday evening program, the show included silent movie narrations, song and dance numbers, and comedy skits aimed at a family audience. It was the first TV comedy series to feature guest appearances from well known performers and personalities. Frank Sinatra was the first performer to get hit with a pie from "Nut-at-the-Door."

HENNESY!
CBS, APRIL 23, 1962
Cast: Lt. Chick Hennesy: Jackie Cooper, Martha: Abby Dalton, Shaffer: Roscoe Karns, Max: Henry Kulky

Naval dentist Lt. Hennesy tries to get Soupy to perform for the kids at the naval hospital.

THE SOUPY SALES SHOW!

SYNDICATED, WEEKDAY AFTERNOONS AND EVENINGS: SEPTEMBER 7, 1964–
SEPTEMBER 3, 1966
SATURDAY MORNINGS AND EVENINGS: SEPTEMBER 12, 1964–SEPTEMBER 4, 1966
Head Puppeteer/Comedy Asistant: Frank Nastasi

Similar to the Friday night show, this version features "The Adventures of Philo Kevetch," a parody of TV crime dramas. Philo Kvetch (Soupy) is a bumbling police detective trying to capture the evil and mysterious crime boss the Mask (also usually played by Soupy). Other characters include: Onions Oregano, the Mask's henchman, and Bruno the Killer Ape, both played by Frank Nastasi. The other members of the Mask's gang are played by various guests. On one episode former "Bowery Boy" Huntz Hall plays the Mask's dumbell son.

This show also features new characters: Peaches, Soupy's girlfriend (played by Frank Nastasi at the front door of Soupy's house, wearing the sleeve of a dress; Soupy plays Peaches in drag in pre-filmed segments); Bessie and Bertha, the elephants; and Reba and Hobart, the elderly couple who live inside Sales's potbelly stove. The show also features performances by popular rock musicians and singers.

THE 38TH ANNUAL MACY'S THANKSGIVING DAY PARADE

NBC, THURSDAY, NOVEMBER 26, 1964
Hosts: Betty White and Lorne Greene
Parade Guests: Soupy Sales, "Capt. Bob" Cottle, Fred Gwynne, Al Lewis, Fess Parker, the Radio City Music Hall Rockettes and Ballet Co., and the New York City Light Opera Co.

JUST FOR FUN

WNEW TV, CHANNEL 5, NEW YORK, SATURDAY MORNING, APRIL 10, 1965
Host: Sonny Fox

Soupy appears in "The Mystery Guest" segment.

THE 39TH ANNUAL MACY'S THANKSGIVING DAY PARADE

NBC, THURSDAY, NOVEMBER 25, 1965
Hosts and performers: Betty White, Lorne Greene
Parade Guests: Soupy Sales, Paul Anka , Jane Morgan, Bill Baird

THE 15TH ANNUAL CELEBRITY PARADE
FOR UNITED CEREBAL PALSY

WOR, CHANNEL 9, NEW YORK: SATURDAY, JANUARY 15, 1966, 10:30 P.M.–SUNDAY,
JANUARY 16,1966, 5:30 P.M.
Hosts: Jane Pickens Langley, William B. Williams, and Soupy Sales

THE JERRY LEWIS MUSCULAR DYSTROPHY
LABOR DAY TELETHON

SUNDAY, SEPTEMBER 4, 1966–MONDAY, SEPTEMBER 5, 1966
Local Hosts: Soupy Sales and Sonny Fox

THE 40TH ANNUAL MACY'S THANKSGIVING DAY PARADE

NBC, THURSDAY, NOVEMBER 24, 1966
Hosts: Betty White, Lorne Greene
Parade Guests: Soupy Sales, racecar driver Jack Brabham, Wilyne Newton, Bruce Yarnell, and Franciose Hardy

THE PIED PIPER OF ASTROWORLD

ABC, SATURDAY, DECEMBER 28, 1968, 11:00 A.M.

Host/Performer: Soupy Sales
Guest Performers: Leslie Gore, the First Edition, the Singing Boys of Houston, the Marching Mustang Band of Houston, and the Muppets

While taking the kids of Hamlin on a hike, the Pied Piper (Soupy Sales) and the kids find themselves lost in Astroworld Amusement Park in Houston, Texas. Soupy performs songs with Leslie Gore, the First Edition, and the Muppets, while trying to round up the kids and return them to Hamlin.

THE NEW WHAT'S MY LINE?

SYNDICATED, WEEKDAY AFTERNOONS AND EVENINGS: SEPTEMBER 9, 1968– APRIL 3, 1972; WEEKDAY AFTERNOONS OCTOBER 3, 1972–OCTOBER 4,1974

Hosts: Wally Brunier And Larry Blyden
Panelists: Soupy Sales, Anita Gillette, Arlene Francis, Bennett Cerf, and Gene Rayburn
Announcers: Johnny Olson and Chet Gould

A panel of well-known performers and personalities question each contestant in order to correctly guess their unusual occupation. The panel (while blindfolded) also tries to find out the identity of the "Mystery Guest," a well-known performer or personality.

THE SOUPY SALES SHOW!

CBS, SUNDAY, AUGUST 30, 1970, 9:00 P.M.

Guest performers: Yvone Wilder, Paula Kelly, Tommy Boyce, Bobby Hart, Art Metrano, and the Don Ellis Orchestra

Comedy skits and musical numbers aimed at an adult audience.

SOUPY SALES SPECIAL

WABC, CHANNEL 7, NEW YORK SUNDAY NIGHT, SEPTEMBER 9, 1973

Head Pupeteer/Comedy Asistant: Clyde Adler
Guest performers: Tony Orlando and Dawn, Marsha Hunt, and Kent Smith
Theme song composed and arranged by Bill Snyder

A program based on Soupy and Clyde's ABC-TV comedy show. Soupy performs his jokes, puns, song and dance numbers, comedy skits, and introduces the new rock singing team of Tony Orlando and Dawn. Broadcast in color.

WAY OUT GAMES!

(PILOT) CBS, SATURDAY, JANUARY 10, 1976, 1:00 P.M.

Hosts: Soupy Sales and Joanna Kerns .

Soupy and Joanna lead high school gym classes from all over the USA and Puerto Rico in zany stunts to see which high school gym class is the most fit. The show was taped before a live audience in Palm Springs, California. CBS picked up the show for its 1976 fall schedule, but the hosting job was given to former *Wonderama* and *Just For Fun!* host Sonny Fox.

JUNIOR ALMOST ANYTHING GOES!

ABC, Saturday Afternoon, September 11, 1976–January 8, 1977
Play-by-play Announcer: "Fast Eddie" Alexander

Soupy, along with "celebrity coaches" (well-known performers and personalities), lead high school gym classes in zany stunts to prove which gym class is the fittest. The winning team wins college scholarship money and a color TV set for their school.

SHA NA NA!

Syndicated, September 11, 1976–September 18, 1981
Performers: "Bowzer," "Denny," "Donny," "Lenny," "Jocko," "Dirty Dan," "Screaming Scott," "Santinni," Avery Schreiber, Soupy Sales, Jane Dulo
Announcer: Pamela Myers.

Soupy and the rock group Sha Na Na perform vintage rock 'n' roll tunes and comedy skits against the backdrop of a inner-city neighborhood and a makeshift basement clubhouse. Soupy appeared on the show first as a wisecracking cop and later on in the series as "Igor," the attendant of the Sha Na Na Clubhouse.

THE ABC TV FUNSHINE FESTIVAL

ABC, Thanksgiving Day, November 25, 1976, 11:30 a.m.
Host: Soupy Sales

Soupy and a group of actors (dressed up as Hanna Barbera's most popular cartoon characters: Tom and Jerry, Scooby Doo, Dynomutt, Jabberjaw, etc.) perform comedy skits, while introducing reruns of *Junior Almost Anything Goes!, The Tom & Jerry Grape Ape Mumbley Show, Jabberjaw, The Scooby Doo/Dynomutt Hour, The Kroft Supershow,* and *The Oddball Couple!*

THE WACKO SATURDAY PREVIEW!

CBS, Thursday, September 8, 1977, 8:00 p.m.
Hosts: Soupy Sales, Loretta Swit, Julie McWhirter, Charlie Fleischer, Bo Kaprell, Jim Backus, the Slyvers, Carol Burnett, Gary Owens, Jonathan Harris, Marty Allen, Harry Nillson, and the Dwight Witty Band

Soupy and the cast members of "Wacko" perform comedy skits and musical numbers to help introduce the new CBS-TV, 1977 Saturday morning schedule of kids shows.

WONDERAMA

Syndicated, Christmas morning, December 25, 197,7 7:00 a.m.
Host/Performer: Bob McCallister

On his final broadcast, Bob McCallister screens videoclips of his show's past ten years and reminices with guests, Mason Reese, Soupy Sales, Joe Raposo, Robert Merrill, Marvin Hamlisch, Don Kirshner, and Van McCoy.

THIS IS YOUR LIFE EMMY

WNEW, channel 5, New York: Sunday, April 30, 1978, 8:00 p.m.
Host: Ralph Edwards

Guests: Carol Channing, Soupy Sales, Immogene Coca , Larry Lester And Dagmar, Archbishop Fulton L. Sheen, James Earl Jones, Barbera Feldon, Tony Curtis , Arthur Godfrey, Betsy Palmer, Ralph Edwards, Soupy Sales, Henry Morgan, and others.

THE NEW SOUPY SALES SHOW
WEEKDAY AFTERNOONS: FEBRUARY 5, 1979–FRIDAY, MARCH 9, 1979
Head Puppeteer/Comedy Asistant: Clyde Adler
Other Comedy Assistants : Bo Kaprell and Marty Brill

Format simular to the previous Soupy Sales shows that aired on ABC and WNEW in New York. This version was in color and featured a new comedy skit: "The Adventures Of Soupyman," a spoof of the feature length Superman movies, where "Clark Bent" (Soupy), a newspaper reporter fights crime as "Soupyman." Clyde Adler plays the editor-in-chief of the newspaper.

THE CBS TV FESTIVAL OF LIVELY ARTS FOR YOUNG PEOPLE MAKE EM' LAUGH! A YOUNG PEOPLE'S COMEDY CONCERT!
CBS, SUNDAY, NOVEMBER 25, 1979, 5:00 P.M.
Co-Hosts: Soupy Sales, Tom Bosley, Jim MacGeorge, Chuck McCann, Skiles and Henderson,
Norm Crosby, Rip Taylor, Bob Shields, the Hudson Brothers, Pamela Myers, and the
Muppets Kermit the Frog and Fozzy Bear.

Taped before a live audience of kids at the Mayfair Music Hall in Santa Monica, California. Tom Bosley, Soupy, and a group of talented comedy performers perform skits to demonstrate to the kids in the theater and at home "what comedy is all about." Soupy Sales plays a zany court jester, who engages Tom Bosley in some witty banter. Later Sales tries to hit Bosley with one of his shaving cream pies, but Soupy gets it in the end.

SATURDAY SUPERCADE
CBS, SATURDAY MORNING AND AFTERNOON, SEPTEMBER 17, 1983–SATURDAY, AUGUST 24, 1985

Cartoons relate the misadventures of characters from these popular video games of the 1980s. Soupy is the voice of Donkey Kong.

FORTY YEARS OF FINE TUNING
WNEW TV, CHANNEL 5, NEW YORK: THURSDAY NIGHT, SEPTEMBER 6, 1984
REPEAT BROADCAST SATURDAY NIGHT, DECEMBER 8, 1984, 8:00- P.M.
Narrator/Interviewer: Carrol O'Connor
Co-Hosts /narrators: Richard Kiley, Peggey Anne Ellis, Rosemary Clooney, Robert Merrill,
Joe Raposo, Tony Metola, Mel Torme, Grace Carney, Earl Hammond, David Suskind,
Joyce Davidson Suskind, Bill Boggs, Betty Furness, Skitch Henderson, Gene Rayburn,
Mike Wallace, Clay Felker, David Frost, Gabe Pressman, Ed Koch, John Roland, Roxie
Roker, Bill McCreary, Marion Etoile Watson, Judy Licht, Sandy Becker, Soupy Sales,
Fred Scott, Chuck McCann, Johnny Olson, Don Hastings, Sonny Fox, Dr. T. Thomas
Goldsmith, Sid Caesar, Morey Amsterdam, Edie Adams, Dennis James, Harry Coyle,
Archbishop John J. O'Connor, Eli Bergman, Chris Schenkel and Bill Mazer

In this two hour 40th anniversary tribute to WABD/WNEW TV channel 5, New York, Soupy Sales and others discuss their successful years as channel 5's most memorable kids-TV hosts/performers.

EYEWITNESS NEWS: A TRIBUTE TO THE GOLDEN AGE OF NYC TV
WABC, CHANNEL 7, NEW YORK, MONDAY–FRIDAY, MARCH 11–15, 1989
Host: Joel Siegel

A weeklong tribute to the 50th anniversary of New York City's most popular and original TV broadcasts.

On Monday, March 11, 1989, Soupy Sales, Chuck McCann, and Sonny Fox, recall their most memorable years in kids TV.

On Wednesday, March 13, 1989, Soupy recalls a mishap during a beer commcerial on his late night comedy/variety TV show *Soupy's On!* that aired not in New York City, but on WXYZ TV channel 7, in Detroit, back in 1953.

EYEWITNESS NEWS: TELEVISION LOST AND FOUND!

WABC, CHANNEL 7, NEW YORK, MONDAY–FRIDAY, MAY 17–21, 1993
Host: Joel Siegel.

Rare kinescopes and videotapes of TV shows, long thought to be lost. On Monday, May 17, 1993, Soupy recalls how former WNEW technician Ken DeGruchey found and salvaged the kinescopes of his New York-based TV comedy show. On Thursday, May 20, 1993, Soupy reminices about his years as New York's most popular kids' TV host.

PALISADES AMUSEMENT PARK: A CENTURY OF FOND MEMORIES!

PBS, MARCH 14, 1998, 8:00 P.M.
Produced by Ken Burns
Guests: Soupy Sales, Bill Britten, Walter Cronkite, John Sebastian, "Cousin Brucie" Morrow, Steve Clayton, Sonny Fox, Vince Gargulio, Sol Abrams, Marti Stevens, John Rinaldi, Freddie Cannon, Gerald Calabreese, John Winkler, Nick and Anna Corbiscello, Jan Lewinter, Ann Mcaskill, Dr. Arthur Shapiro, the voice of Mrs. Gladys, Shelly Rosenthal, and Buddy Hackett

Soupy recalls his visits to New Jersey's most famous fun spot: Palisades Amusement Park.

NY TV: BY THE PEOPLE WHO MADE IT!

WNET, CHANNEL 13, NEW YORK, MONDAY NIGHT DECEMBER 14, 1998, 9:00 P.M.
Hosts: Walter Cronkite and Al Roker.
Guests: Soupy Sales, Chuck McCann, John Zacherley, Sonny Fox, Jack Lemmon, Milton Berle, Jeff Kissloff, Al Lewis, Charolette Rae, Nipsey Russell, Rod Steiger, Ossie Davis, Ruby Dee, Leslie Uggams, Henry Winkler, Joel Grey, Hughs Downs, Woody Allen, Tony Randall, Thomas W. Sarnoff, Steve Allen, Martin Mayer, Rosemary Rice, Dick Van Patten, Dick Cavett, Sid Caesar, Max Wilk, Dick Wolf, Jac Venza, Fred Silverman, Harve Bennett, Nancy Marchand, Sid Lumet, Howard Davis, Howard Meltzer, Herb Holmes, Agnes Nixon, Jerry ver Dorn, James McAdams, Hildy Parks, Alexander Edie Adams, Bill Lawrence, Ed Koch, Gabe Pressman, Mike Wallace, Mary Stuart, Mary Alice Dwyer Dobbin, Tom Freston, Irving Needle, Kitty Carlisle Hart, Art Moore, Chris Schenkle, Dick Schaap, Dede Allen, Sol Negrin, Rae Pichon, Walter Wager, Ward Chamberlin, Alvin Cooperman, Bill Boggs, Joe Franklin, Jeff Folmsbee, Lorne Michaels, Paul Rauch, Newton Minow, Larry Gelbart, Maury Povich, and Ed Herlihy

In this two hour tribute to New York's best TV shows, Soupy Sales recalls his experiences as New York's most popular kids' TV host.

SUNDAY: TODAY IN NY!

WNBC TV, CHANNEL 4, NEW YORK, SUNDAY, FEBRUARY 7, 1999, 7:00 A.M.
Hosts: Al Roker, Felica Taylor, Soupy Sales, and Sonny Fox

Soupy Sales recalls his experiences as one of New York's most popular kids' TV performers.

TELEVISION CREDITS

The Tonight Show
The Merv Griffin Show
The Mike Douglas Show
The Arsenio Hall Show
The Sally Jessy Raphael Show
Later with Bob Costas
Good Morning America
McKeever and the Colonel
The Ed Sullivan Show
The Pyramid Game Shows
The Johnny Cash Show
The Barbara McNair Show
Bloopers and Practical Jokes
The Judy Garland Show
The Globetrotter's Special

Everybody's Talking
Hollywood Squares
To Tell the Truth
Snap Judgement
What's My Line?
I've Got a Secret
Celebrity Family Feud
The Kraft Music Hall
The Carol Burnett Show
Win, Lose, or Draw
You're Putting Me On
Name Droppers
The Joan Rivers Show
My Favorite Jokes
The Edie Adams Show

Sha-Na-Na
True Blue
Hennesy
Route 66
Password
The Match Game
The Real McCoys
Burke's Law
Ensign O'Toole
ABC Night Life
First Impressions
Saturday Night Live
Evening at the Improv
Third Degree
The Bob Hope Show

MOTION PICTURES

Two Little Bears (20th Century Fox)
Critics Choice (Warner Brothers)
Birds Do It (Columbia)
Don't Push—I'll Charge When I'm Ready (Universal)
. . . And God Spoke (Live Entertainment, Inc.)
Everything's George (Independent)
Behind the Seams (Independent)
Palmer's Pick-Up (Independent)
The Holy Man (Touchstone)
JT Foster's Little Bit of Lipstick (Independent)
This Train (Independent)
Naked and Laughing (Independent)

STOCK

Hellzapoppin' (Expo '67, Montreal)
Star Spangled Girl (Mineola Playhouse, Long Island, NY)
Finian's Rainbow (Light City Opera, Atlanta, GA)
High Button Shoes (Kenley Players, Columbus, Warren and Dayton, OH)
Sugar (Sacramento Music Circus, CA)
Come Live with Me (Cherry County Playhouse, Traverse City, MI; Showboat Dinner Theater, Tampa, Saint Petersburg, FL; Windmill Dinner Theater, Houston, TX; Granny's Dinner Theater, Dallas, TX)
Visit to a Small Planet (Cherry County Playhouse, Traverse City, MI)
Pajama Game (San Bernadino Light Civic Opera, CA)
Heyday of Burlesque (Sacramento Music Circus, CA; Candlewood Playhouse, New Fairfield, CT)

acKnoWLeDGements

I'd like to thank all those who helped me with this book, and that includes those who gave their time to share their memories: Charlie Cook, Bill Cravens, Betty Ann Keen, Ernie Salvatore, Dave Usher, Crispin Cioe, Larry Storch, Peter Strand, Mark Evanier, Paul Dver, Ray D'ariano, Gene Klavan, Perry Gardner, Uncle Floyd Vivino, Joyce and Jack Keller, Jim Reina, Bob Stewart, and Al Roker.

I'd also like to thank the folks at Rhino Records for reissuing a CD compilation of my record albums as well as three videotapes of *The Soupy Sales Show* highlights. This book would not have been possible without the untiring work of my wonderful, indefatigable agent, June Clark, the gang at M. Evans, including George DeKay, my editor, PJ Dempsey, Harry McCullogh and Amy Koch, and Shelly Cofield for her administrative help.

I'd also like to thank Jean-Pierre Trebot, Frank Capitelli, Barry Dougherty, Michael Caputo, Mickey Freeman, Joe Gelber, Freddie Roman, Mark Shatsky and Jack L. Green, and the the rest of my pals at the Friars Club, as well as Jules Feiler, Debbie Studer and Derek Meade, Richard Jerome, Elliot Novak, and Kevin Butler.

A special thanks to Frank Nastassi, White Fang, Black Tooth, Pookie, and the rest of my gang.

And, oh yes, I certainly can't forget to mention my wonderful wife, Trudy, who still laughs at all (okay, almost all) of my jokes.

Also, my oldest and dearest friend, Gid Gilliam. Hunt Sales, Harold and Dodi Frankel, Mark and Matt Miller, John Houvouras, Clint McElroy, George Mallot, Jean Dean, Leonard Keen, Jim Casto, Bob Withers, Don Kleppe, John Mandt, John Mandt Jr., Bill Nimmo, Nick Clooney, Dagmar, Dick Clark, Marcia Ball, Milton Berle, Terry Gibbs, Pat O'Haire, Dick Capri, Charlie Callas, Bobby Ramsen, Sal Richards, Harold Rand, Bobby Shields, Marlin Swing, Richard Miller, Bob Hope, Peter Vartiainen, Dick O'Leary, Joey Reynolds, Regis Philbin, Ann Marie Schmidt, Dauod David Williams, Rothschild, Topal, Miller and Kraft, Cindy Adams, Liz Smith, Jeffery Lyons, J. Preston Carson, Jack Supman, Joe Franklin, Dave King, Dr. Linda Carroll, Janet Oseroff, Steve Duboff, Bernie Ilson, Burton Rocks, Lawrence Rocks, Fred Elias Jr., Aralee Strange, Ray Boes, Elizabeth Harris, Mark Simone, J.T. Foster, Ric Bohy, Al Sussman, Barry Mitchell, Scott Shannon, Dan Taylor, Steve Gruberg, Vic Gelb, Ottie Adkins, Burt DuBrow, Richy Victor, Ed Hider, Marti Scholl, Paul Huber, Aldo Paletti, Jim Hassing, Dick Purtin, Tom Ryan, Martin Brandike, Ken Calvert, Jimmy Launce, Mort Crim, Joe Schmidt, Mason Weaver, Betty Lou Peterson, Neil Rubin, Tim Kiska, Elayna Nacantha, Ernie Harwell, Wayne Stevens, Paul W. Smith, Denny McLaine, Bob Hines, Paul Stanley, Mort Zieve, Toni and John Genetti, Gertz Kuntzman, Pinky Kravitz, Jerry Blavet, David Spatz, Bill Lucas, Del Jack, Jim Buck, Sid Bernstein, Howard Rosenberg, Richard Duryea, Al and Arlene Gitt, Judy D'Angelis, Bruce Leonard, Dale Parsons, Marv Welch, Joel Bogarad, Mary Milton, John Socia, Pat Cooper, Jackie Kallen, Pat and Joe Moran, Egon Domler, and Bob Factor

And most importantly, Charles Salzberg, a tremendous writer and a great friend, whose talent, patience, and devotion to this project overwhelmed me. All I can say, from the bottom of my heart, Charles, is thank you!